ARCHITECTURE
AND OBJECTS

ART AFTER NATURE

Giovanni Aloi and Caroline Picard, Series Editors

Architecture and Objects
Graham Harman

Eco Soma: Pain and Joy in Speculative Performance Encounters
Petra Kuppers

Art and Posthumanism: Essays, Encounters, Conversations
Cary Wolfe

ARCHITECTURE AND OBJECTS

Art
after
Nature

GRAHAM HARMAN

University of Minnesota Press
MINNEAPOLIS ■ LONDON

Published by the University of Minnesota Press
111 Third Avenue South, Suite 290
Minneapolis, MN 55401-2520
http://www.upress.umn.edu

ISBN 978-1-5179-0852-2 (hc)
ISBN 978-1-5179-0853-9 (pb)

A Cataloging-in-Publication record for this book is available from the Library of Congress.

Printed in the United States of America on acid-free paper

The University of Minnesota is an equal-opportunity educator and employer.

28 27 26 25 24 23 22   10 9 8 7 6 5 4 3 2 1

Architecture, the noble offspring of judgment and fancy, was gradually formed in the most polite and knowing countries of Asia, Egypt, Greece, and Italy. It was cherished and esteemed by the most flourishing states and most renowned princes, who with vast expense improved and brought it to perfection. It seems, above all other arts, peculiarly conversant about order, proportion, and symmetry. May it not therefore be supposed, on all accounts, most likely to help us to some rational notion of the *je ne sais quoi* in beauty?

GEORGE BERKELEY, *ALCIPHRON*

CONTENTS

INTRODUCTION

WHY A BOOK CALLED *ARCHITECTURE AND OBJECTS,* ASIDE FROM the fact that the author is a philosopher of objects who has recently gone to work at a leading architecture school? If architecture is concerned with buildings, then a reader might wonder why this is a more pressing topic than any other—say, *Agriculture and Objects,* or perhaps *Military Science and Objects.* One reason is that architecture bears directly on the object-oriented ontology (OOO) principle of "aesthetics as first philosophy," a topic of considerable discussion in my writing.[1] But perhaps a better reason stems from David Ruy's thesis that architecture provides human beings with their primary sense of reality.[2] Whoever you are, much of your life has no doubt unfolded in towns and cities—artificial and historically recent environments that tighten their grip on the planet with every passing year, despite recent flight to the countryside during the ongoing Covid pandemic. Those of our memories not tied to urban areas are still largely confined to the interiors of buildings, and even outdoor experience features heavily sculpted landscapes, intensively crafted public spaces, and organized national parks. If we turn away from all this and flee toward raw nature, we nonetheless find that geographical features as "natural" as the Mississippi River bear little resemblance to the condition in which they were found.

If architecture is the primary medium in which human existence takes place, it cannot fail to be one of the most relevant philosophical topics. Though we might be tempted to speak of architecture as the first virtual reality, it would be more accurate to call it the first *augmented* reality, since it does not dispense with prehuman light, wind, and bedrock. Instead, it channels or grafts itself onto these forces, obstructing or harnessing them as needed. Here a wide field of inquiry opens up, one potentially much wider than the usual scope of architecture as a discipline. But since the present book is a short one, I propose to deal with just two questions: (1) What is the relation between architecture and philosophy? (2) What is the relation between architecture and art? If we make headway on each of these topics, everything else will fall into place.

What is the relation between architecture and philosophy? Over the past half century there has been a remarkable openness of architecture to philosophy, if less often in the other direction. Yet there have been complaints about this from architects, as in the following ironic Twitter thread by Fred Scharmen:

- Architects & Philosophy: (1) Lévi-Strauss liked signifiers, so let's make things with historical resonance.
- Architects & Philosophy: (2) Derrida liked difference, so let's make things that clash and collide.
- Architects & Philosophy: (3) Deleuze & Guattari like[d] smooth continuities, so let's make things that blend and fold.
- Architects & Philosophy: (4) Graham Harman likes inexhaustible objects, so let's make mysterious things with variable outlines.[3]

The main omission is Heidegger, though it is easy enough to add him to the list: "(5) Heidegger liked the openness of human beings to Being itself, so let's make things that emphasize natural sunlight, wood, and stone." But before we applaud this comical series too quickly, consider the possible counterpunch: "(6) Fred Scharmen likes mocking architects who find inspiration in philosophy, so let's focus on internal disciplinary craft and proclaim our solidarity with the poor." Irony is a double-edged sword, easily wielded against its user in turn.

That aside, Scharmen's remarks could be read in two different ways, as indeed they have been. In a cataclysmic sense, the tweets could be read as follows: "The architectural use of philosophies will always go astray into overly literal applications, so let's put an end to this endless sham and get back to doing architecture on its own terms."[4] Yet this sort of maximalist antiphilosophy program seems insufficiently motivated. Throughout its history architecture has been deeply entangled with neighboring and distant disciplines, ranging from sculpture and religion to economics and warcraft to banking and the construction of border walls. Indeed, architects on the whole display an unusual degree of intellectual curiosity and are known to be experimenters almost to a fault. Hence it is unclear why philosophy alone should be banished from their sphere of interests. But in a more moderate sense, Scharmen's tweets might simply mean: "Some architects have been overly literal in adapting philosophical ideas to the tasks of design. Let's avoid doing this." Designers could then take this as a cautionary note and try to avoid any careless importation of ideas from philosophy, as in the unsettling use of crooked windows to celebrate Derridean *différance,* or the possibly excessive use of folded shapes in honor of Deleuze.[5] However bland this more muted warning may sound, it raises the important question of how to distinguish between overly literal and properly architectural appropriation of philosophical insights.

What is the relation between architecture and art? Of chief interest here is the concept of "formalism," which has multiple meanings in each of these fields. Let's begin with the visual art sense of the term. Like anything else, aesthetic objects can be considered either as cut off from their surroundings or as elements and expressions of those surroundings. Let's call the first approach "formalist" and the second "antiformalist," and take the German philosophers Immanuel Kant and G. W. F. Hegel (and his Frankfurt School heirs) as the respective mascots of these two positions. The central concern of Kant's philosophy is the autonomy of distinct domains that must not be improperly mixed; on this basis, he ranks as the central figure of ontological, ethical, and aesthetic formalism.[6] For Kant, just as the thing-in-itself is severed from appearance and set apart from all direct human access, and just as ethical acts must be considered apart from their consequences, so too are artworks cut off from all personal preference and conceptual explanation.[7] By contrast, Hegel is all about relations: everything emerges from a total historical process, so that art is just another shape of spirit jostling in the same crowd as politics, religion, and commerce, each of them expressing a wider style of the age.[8]

This basic dispute still remains lively, even when it is dismissed as tedious and old-fashioned. Although antiformalism currently has the upper hand, due largely to the dominant status of emancipatory politics in contemporary intellectual life, there is much to be said for a strong dose of formalism. This is not because nothing relates to anything else, but because nothing relates to *everything* else. Different disciplines in the same historical moment do not always strike the same chord but often move at variable speeds in oblique directions; any evidence of a shared *Zeitgeist* is usually limited to parallels in three or four fields at most, and time-consuming labor and extensive caveats are needed to show even this much. In other words, there are no grounds for positing a general historical atmosphere in which everything moves together in unison. The reason for giving formalist attention to autonomous individuals is not to valorize preexistent physical units that exclude all relations but to emphasize that while every object is composed of relations between its parts, and is engaged in a certain number of relations, no object dissolves into affinities with everything else in the cosmos. The relations that play into any object are shadowed by a definite degree of closure. The hydrogen and oxygen that compose a molecule of water do not permit other atoms to join and disturb their union. The pair "Deleuze and Guattari" is just as real an object as either of these thinkers in isolation, yet it resists easy expansion into "Deleuze and Guattari and Napoleon." This same exclusivity holds for the Golden Horde, the Five Mafia Families of New York, and the Sword in the Stone. Any object consists of smaller elements while repelling—at least provisionally—whatever else has not yet been made to belong. Even the most "site-specific" works of art and architecture are highly selective as to which aspects of their sites they deem relevant; in this respect, a degree of formalism is always employed even by those who denounce the term.[9] The true formalist principle is not that objects do not relate, but that these relations are always limited in number, and that human or nonhuman labor is needed to create them.[10]

Although Kant is surely the founder of modern formalism, he is too strict on this topic, forbidding any interaction between artwork and environment at all. He is already suspicious of the beauty of humans and horses, which he takes to be hopelessly entangled with ulterior motives: admiration for a beautiful human body seems dangerously close to lust, while awe before a beautiful horse seems connected with the utility of the animal's speed, so that both count as "merely [accessory] beauty."[11] More important here, another target of Kant's suspicion is the architect: "In architecture the main concern is what *use* is to be made of the artistic object, and this is a use to which the aesthetic ideas are confined."[12] Kant does not mean this as a compliment. As he sees it, for an aesthetic object to be useful is no better than for an ethical action to be useful; in both cases, the purity of the thing is lost. We may well admire an architect's concern with the subtlest features of a project site, the sociopolitical aspects of a design brief, or the rhetorical skill with which a city council is persuaded to commission a radical project. But for a formalist philosophy devoted to the autonomy of art from anything else, the status of architecture would seem to be relatively low. That is Kant's position, though my conclusion will be the opposite.[13] A certain amount of autonomy is inevitable simply because everything is what it is rather than everything else too, despite Jacques Derrida's forays into disputing the classical law of identity.[14] Nonetheless, Kant's version of autonomy is also hopelessly narrow, and architecture is uniquely positioned to show us why. This is why it must now take the lead in aesthetic theory, just as poetry, tragedy, and cinema have done for other philosophies at other times.

As mentioned, this book is guided by the double question of architecture's relation to philosophy on the one hand and to art on the other. But already these themes have transmuted into questions that go well beyond that of disciplinary boundaries. To ask about architecture and philosophy is to raise the more general question of how to translate content from one genre or medium into another without clumsy literalism. To ask about architecture and art is to raise the issue of Kantian formalism, and whether architecture—which cannot fail to be useful, under penalty of turning into sculpture or semiotics—is capable of autonomy from its surroundings at all.

The ideas in this book are deeply indebted to numerous architects and theorists, both my immediate colleagues and others. But one debt in particular needs to be registered here. My first proposal for this book received an unusually thorough and generous critique from Aron Vinegar of the University of Oslo. As a result of his comments, which, among other things, suggested that I be more ambitious in my coverage of themes, the plans for this book were modified almost beyond recognition, as was the title of the book. As if that were not enough, he provided another, equally lengthy review of the completed manuscript, which again prompted substantial changes to the final book. I thank Vinegar heartily for that rarest of gifts: the feedback of a critic who actually wishes me well.

I am also grateful to others who provided crucial feedback on the first draft: Giovanni Aloi, Ferda Kolatan, Pieter Martin, Caroline Picard, Peter Trummer, Gonzalo Vaillo, Jordi Vivaldi Piera, and Simon Weir, along with an anonymous second reviewer for the University of Minnesota Press. Mark Foster Gage, with whom it was my good fortune to co-teach a studio at Yale University, went so far as to provide a page-by-page commentary on the initial draft. Joseph Bedford of Virginia Tech did the same and also prepared an invaluable PDF with nearly twenty articles he found relevant to my central claims, many of them cited in what follows. My assistant Khosro Salarian provided sage counsel from an early date and also sent many useful articles my way. Micah Tewers suggested a specific reordering of chapters and sections that I have largely adopted, with a few additional changes. I also profited greatly from conversations and e-mail exchanges with Michael Benedikt.

Theo Lorenz and Tanja Siems were the first to invite me to speak at an architectural school: at the AA in London in 2007. Yet it is unlikely that I would have landed more permanently in this world if not for David Ruy, a long-lost undergraduate classmate who resurfaced at just the right moment to insist that my philosophy was of relevance to his field. From there one thing led to another, and in 2016 I left the American University in Cairo for the Southern California Institute of Architecture in Los Angeles, a bastion of aesthetic gamblers too little known outside the design community. SCI-Arc director Hernán Díaz Alonso and vice director John Enright took a chance and added me to their team, with a key assist from undergraduate director Tom Wiscombe. I hope they do not regret it.

In a life of many travels, this has nonetheless been my first chance to live near the ocean. As others have noted before me, sea air does something new and important to the writer's brain. My wife, Necla, has been with me every morning, enjoying the Pacific winds.

1 ARCHITECTS AND THEIR PHILOSOPHERS

IT WAS ALBENA YANEVA WHO BROUGHT ACTOR-NETWORK theory, or ANT, into its closest contact with architecture so far. ANT has long been a burgeoning method in the social sciences, where it boasts tens of thousands of practitioners.[1] Among its key slogans is "Follow the actors," meaning that rather than deploying such vague and sweeping concepts as "capital," "society," or "the state," ANT focuses on all the various entities that go into composing a given situation, including those that might seem trivial. An ANT account of a laboratory, for instance, might focus on the blackboard or the garbage can in the room as much as on the episte-mological debates that take place there. This theory's focus on individuals of all scales and types helped make it one of the major inspirations for OOO (pronounced "Triple O"), with two key differences. First, for ANT an actor is—by definition—composed entirely of its actions, with no hid-den substance or surplus lying behind its explicit deeds.[2] For OOO, by contrast, there is a real object: a concealed reserve never exhausted by its sum total of actions. Second, ANT

allows for no difference between an object and its own qualities, thereby tacitly accepting the philosopher David Hume's
view that a tree or an apple is nothing more than a "bundle
of qualities," a view that OOO explicitly rejects.[3] These two
points play a key role in the present book, as they do in all
writing done in a OOO vein.

In any case, Yaneva deserves most of the credit for bringing ANT to bear on architectural theory. This is most obvious
in her book *The Making of a Building,* for which she embedded
herself in Rem Koolhaas's Office for Metropolitan Architecture in Rotterdam, as OMA tried but failed to win the competition to renovate New York's Whitney Museum of American Art. Her book frames architectural works as ongoing
dynamic processes rather than completed products frozen in
an instant of time. Those who prefer a more condensed sample of Yaneva's method might turn to a compact 2019 piece
coauthored with Brett Mommersteeg. Here the authors question whether an individual building can ever be the proper
unit of architectural analysis. They worry about the notion
of buildings as "abstract, immutable, frighteningly lonely
and isolated from the world."[4] Along with the isolation of
buildings as finished units, they are bothered by the purported solitude of the solo genius architect: "Can we believe
that only one man deserves to be [in the] picture next to the
magnificent unity of a static oeuvre?"[5] If we look instead at
what the authors term "architecture-in-the-making," we
find a whole crowd of entities involved in the project, ranging from ecological impact studies and software terminals
to acoustic engineers, zoning boards, and underpaid office
interns.[6] Using further ANT language, Yaneva and Mommersteeg remind us that "a building connects various heterogeneous actors in diverging ways."[7] Bemoaning the old
architectural dualism of form and function, they assert that
"the only way to get out of this dichotomy is to embrace a
relational perspective," thus paying tribute to Alfred North
Whitehead, one of the great philosophical champions of a

relational model of beings.[8] The building is not a noun, but is best treated as a verb.[9] In this way, the authors propose to replace conventional architectural aesthetics with what they call "a symphony of voices."[10]

Now, while I have long been on record as a fan of ANT, the approach to architecture taken in the present book is exactly the opposite of the one adopted by Yaneva and Mommersteeg. No one would deny that a vast and intricate process goes into the design and construction of any architectural project; nor would anyone contest that a building, once finished, has an innumerable multitude of effects on the outside world. Moreover, this is true not just of buildings but of all objects: there is nothing without a backstory, nothing devoid of smaller components, nothing that is not known largely through its impact on its surroundings. What can be disputed—and what I will dispute—is whether dissolving an architectural object both downward into its pieces and upward into its consequences is the right way to do it justice.

The OOO terms for what Yaneva and Mommersteeg propose are "undermining" and "overmining."[11] One of the basic lessons of OOO concerns the shortcomings of any claim to know an object. If someone asks us what something is, there are only two basic possible answers: (1) we can tell them what it is made of, whether compositionally or historically, or (2) we can tell them what it does, whether to other objects or to our own minds and senses. These two operations constitute the sum total of what we call knowledge: without them, the human species would have died a violent early death. In short, "to know" means to analyze an object in terms of the smaller and larger entities with which it is involved. This holds true equally for the theoretical labors of science, the daily operations of practical know-how, and the continual stream of sensorimotor experience in an infant learning to walk. But even so, knowledge does not exhaust the sphere of human cognition. An obvious counterexample is the arts, the realm to which architecture itself in part belongs. It is well known that no artwork can be paraphrased by an explanation of its meaning, and that no building is replaceable by any prose description of its appearance and program. When we try to reduce a building to the complexity of actors that made it possible, we commit two kinds of mistakes. First, not all of the actions or causes that give rise to the building remain important to the building itself. The various human anecdotes and purchasing decisions in a building's history might make for good entertainment, but many of these incidents could have played out differently—or in some cases never happened at all—without there being any noteworthy effect on the final product. Yaneva and Mommersteeg refer to the end observer or user of a building somewhat dismissively as a "tourist."[12] Yet this is true only in the sense that readers of books or citizens in a democracy are also tourists, since they need not be aware of the grisly manner in which "sausages and the law" are actually made, to use Bismarck's famous phrase. Like all objects, a building forgets much of its history, and while this may be regrettable for an archivist, it is simply the reality of what happens with objects in the world.

Second, and more important, a building is like anything else in having emergent properties not found in its compositional or historical components. No detailed account of the history of a building will ever quite give us the building itself. Although Yaneva and Mommersteeg frame their argument as seeking a new kind of aesthetics, to disassemble a building into a swarm of subactors is anything but an aesthetic operation. It might succeed as anthropology or ethnography, or for the purposes of an urban planning task force. But to speak of aesthetics is to speak of the effects of a unified work in tension with its own qualities, not with its internal history and outer effects. As I will argue in this book, the way beyond the usual dualism of form and function is not to dissolve them into a haze of limitless relations but to *de-relationize* both terms. I am aware that this cuts against the grain of contemporary discourse, which favors connection over disjunction, verbs over nouns, process over product, and dynamism over supposed stasis. Yet I am also confident that the reader will be persuaded by the case I present.

As indicated, a building can be "overmined" no less than it can be undermined. This happens when it is treated as having value only in relation to something other than itself, as in another procedure found in both ANT and Alfred North Whitehead's philosophy: the practice of analyzing an object solely in terms of its relations with other objects.[13] The main problem with overmining is that it dissolves a thing into its current set of interactions, or perhaps into the supposed set of all its possible interactions. Such an analysis fails simply because nothing is equal to what it currently does; all things are a partially unexpressed surplus in every moment, more than what the world is able to recognize or appreciate in them. And even if we imagine a thing as equal to all the activities in which it might *conceivably* be involved, such actions are possible only insofar as the thing is a surplus able to support all of its possible uses. One of the central theses of this book is that in their traditional sense, the architectural notions of form and function are both overmining terms. "Form" is usually taken to mean something like the "visual look" of a building, and this reduces it to its appearance to us, thereby hiding the deeper form that makes such appearances possible. Meanwhile, it is even more evident that the idea of function (or program) reduces a building to its relations to specific purposes, thus missing a deeper layer of function that precedes any specific commitments. Let's use the terms "zero-form" and "zero-function" to refer to the de-relationized versions of these two venerable topics of architecture.[14] By taking this step we involve ourselves with formalism and the Kantian notion of autonomy, ideas that already have a well-worn track record in architecture.[15] Nonetheless, in this book I will offer a fresh take on both concepts, as I have already done for the visual arts sense of form in my book *Art and Objects*.

For all its intellectual appeal, ANT has not had a major impact on architecture so far. But other philosophies have had such impacts at various times. Kant and Hegel had tremendous influence on architecture in the nineteenth century, just as they did in nearly all other fields. But in the twentieth and early twenty-first centuries, there are three philosophers who—above all others—have left an imprint on the way architecture is done: Martin Heidegger, Jacques Derrida, and Gilles Deleuze. Let's begin this book by considering each of these cases in turn.

Martin Heidegger

The recent period of architecture's involvement with philosophy began following World War II, as the prewar modernism of the International Style reached the point of crisis that all successful movements eventually do. The situation was addressed in the 1960s in a trio of influential books: Robert Venturi's *Complexity and Contradiction in Architecture,* Aldo Rossi's *The Architecture of the City,* and Manfredo Tafuri's *Theories and History of Architecture.* (Though all three surnames are Italian, Venturi was a native of Philadelphia.) The philosophers who had an impact on architecture at various times from the 1950s through the early 2000s—including Heidegger, Derrida, and Deleuze—shared with these authors various suspicions toward unfettered modern rationalism. They also shared a passionate interest in history, along with the wish to chart a new course without relapsing into pre-Enlightenment modes of thought. If not for this modernist crisis internal to architecture, it is unlikely that architects would have so readily consulted philosophy for new impulses.

We begin with Heidegger, who is widely regarded as the greatest philosopher of the past century despite his involvement with Adolf Hitler and Nazism, a link that only becomes more alarming as new documents are published. Although

Heidegger's influence falls under the general heading of "architectural phenomenology," his relation to phenomenology is famously complicated. This school was founded by his teacher Edmund Husserl, a onetime mathematician whose philosophical work was conducted in a spirit of unapologetic rationalism. Phenomenology, as the term suggests, confines itself to a painstaking description of what is directly given to the mind, in an effort to "bracket" all speculative theories of the real in favor of what is directly evident and therefore unshakable. Among other things, this entails a demotion of scientific theories to the second rank; all science is said to be grounded in the more primary givenness of things to us, the only soil from which explicit knowledge can grow. For instance, we see only the surfaces of objects that are facing us at any given moment, and merely assume that the rest must also be there. Furthermore, most of our words and ideas are "empty intentions" that refer to their objects without those objects becoming fully present either to the senses or to the imagination. Phenomenology in this sense is an effort to pay attention to how reality actually presents itself, rather than relying on inherited prejudice or derivative knowledge as to how the world is.

Husserl had countless followers, and phenomenology is still practiced to this day, though in my view it is compromised by a deep-rooted form of philosophical idealism. Such figures as Maurice Merleau-Ponty, Roman Ingarden, Jean-Paul Sartre, Emmanuel Levinas, and Michel Henry are a small sample of the many important thinkers inspired by Husserl's work. Another influential author, the French philosopher Gaston Bachelard, did not belong to Husserl's line of students but is frequently discussed in architectural phenomenology anyway, due to his sensitive descriptions of space and various physical elements.[16] As so often happens, Husserl's most crucial disciple was also his most rebellious: Heidegger. Despite Heidegger's obvious debt to his teacher, it is fair to say that his philosophy moves in the opposite direction from Husserl's own. Namely, although Husserl asks us to bring any object before our minds in clear and direct presence, Heidegger denies that such a thing is possible. In the eyes of the younger thinker, it is rare for anything to be directly present to our conscious minds at all. For the most part we silently rely on the things of the world without noticing them, except on those rare occasions when they malfunction or otherwise become obtrusive. This comes from the so-called tool-analysis of Heidegger's masterwork *Being and Time,* which happens to be the subject of my own first book.[17] As a rule, these entities remain concealed from us—as does Being itself, the ultimate topic of philosophy. Whenever there is talk of architectural phenomenology there is often some resonance with Merleau-Ponty, who excelled in rich accounts of human perception and embodiment. Yet the ultimate referent of architectural phenomenology is Heidegger, who is less concerned with the sort of lucid rational knowledge that Husserl sought than with the concrete existential situation of humans in their lived environment.[18]

Heidegger's only work dedicated to architecture specifically is the brief essay "Building Dwelling Thinking," originally given as a lecture at a 1951 conference in Darmstadt, Germany, on the postwar housing crisis in that country. Although Heidegger was not very knowledgeable about the field, he at least made an effort to extend his philosophy in that direction, and architects have rewarded his efforts with decades of attentive reading. At the beginning of this work we find a typical sample of Heidegger's oracular late style: "We attain to dwelling, so it seems, only by building. The latter, building, has the former, dwelling, as its goal. Still, not every building is a dwelling. Bridges and hangars, stadiums and power stations are buildings but not dwellings; railway stations and highways, dams and market halls are buildings, but not dwellings."[19] His point about dwelling is not just that we do not reside on bridges or in power stations. More relevant here is Heidegger's lifelong contempt for the efficient products of modern urban society, which he frequently describes as "ontic" rather than ontological: as calculable stockpiles that distract us from the deep concealment of Being itself. As a rule, Heidegger finds positive traces of concealment among Black Forest peasant folk rather than among urbane Berliners. Even more hopeless in his eyes are the technology-adoring Americans and Soviets, both guilty of stripping all mystery from things and reducing them to direct presence. One could easily link such attitudes with his Nazism, though it proves more fruitful to connect them with the core of his philosophy. Rather than calculating and enframing, human works should aim at "preserving and nurturing," addressing what is partly concealed in the world with a degree of poetic tact rather than subjecting reality to a kind of strip-mining quantification.[20]

Along with preserving and nurturing, Heidegger speaks of saving. As he puts it: "Saving the earth does not master the earth and does not subjugate it, which is merely one step from boundless spoliation."[21] In this context "earth" is a technical term, serving as one element of Heidegger's cryptic "fourfold" of earth, sky, gods, and mortals, introduced in 1949.[22] It is my view that Heidegger does not mean earth, sky, gods, and mortals in a literal sense, though most commentators stray in that direction.[23] Instead, the fourfold is a philosophical structure in which "earth" and "gods" refer to two aspects of what is concealed (unity and multiplicity), while "mortals" and "sky" refer in turn to two aspects of that which is present to us (again, unity and multiplicity). For the later Heidegger, the thing is that which "gathers" the fourfold, whereas "object" for him is a pejorative term referring to the thing as reduced to its presence for human thought. Needless to say, he holds that architecture should be concerned with inscrutable fourfold things rather than calculable objects positioned in grid-like Cartesian space.[24] As opposed to space in this objective or measurable sense, human beings are rooted in *place* (or "locale," as the cited translation has it). This positioning in place rather than objective space is precisely what dwelling means: it is "*the basic character* of Being, in keeping with which mortals exist."[25] In closing, Heidegger urges that mortals "build out of dwelling, and think for the sake of dwelling."[26]

While the consequences for architects might seem unclear, it is safe to say that no one under Heidegger's influence would want to design buildings in the International Style, or in any modernist or functionalist spirit at all. Vague though his conception of architecture may be, it is centered in an "authentic" human who shuns premature rationalization and is guided instead by discreet awareness of the partial hiddenness of Being. This is the vision that continues to be developed by phenomenologically inspired architects, including such prominent figures as Kenneth Frampton, Steven Holl, and Alberto Pérez-Gómez. But here I will focus on three others instead, beginning with the Finnish architect Juhani Pallasmaa, whose brief book *The Eyes of the Skin* gives a good summary of his position.

Pallasmaa complains about "retinal" approaches to aesthetics, which harks back to the Dadaism of Marcel Duchamp, though the two figures draw very different lessons from this shared critique. Whereas Duchamp downplays the eye in favor of an art that makes us think, Pallasmaa treats the eye and the mind as two sides of a unified conspiracy against the senses. Contemporary artworks, he says critically, "speak to the intellect and to the conceptualizing capacities instead of addressing the senses and the undifferentiated embodied responses."[27] The concern with "embodiment" clearly owes more to Merleau-Ponty than to Heidegger himself.[28] Foremost among the senses, Pallasmaa contends, is touch: "[It] is the sensory mode that integrates our experience of the world with that of ourselves. Even visual perceptions are fused and integrated into the haptic continuum of the self; my body remembers who I am and where I am located in the world."[29] Preconscious perception is a crucial part of our experience, and includes peripheral no less than direct vision.[30] Even more so than with other forms of art, "a bodily reaction is an inseparable aspect of the experience of architecture."[31] Again striking a Heideggerian note, Pallasmaa laments that "modern architectural theory and critique have a strong tendency to regard space as an immaterial object delineated by surfaces, instead of understanding space in terms of dynamic interactions and interrelations."[32] And just as Heidegger treats being-toward-death as the foremost existential experience of humans, Pallasmaa favors natural materials largely because they wear down over time. As he sees it, modern architecture prefers smooth, glassy, and enameled materials as a way of dodging mortality: "This fear of the traces of wear and age is related to our fear of death."[33]

Among philosophers, the best-known book of architectural phenomenology is surely *Genius Loci,* by the influential Norwegian Christian Norberg-Schulz. As the title of the book suggests, it is less a strictly architectural work than a general anthropology of place, capped by delicious analyses of three distinct urban locales: mysterious Prague, threefold Khartoum, and outdoors-turned-indoors Rome.[34] Ironically, what makes *Genius Loci* such a fascinating test of the relation between architecture and philosophy is that Norberg-Schulz gives the most literalist misreading of Heidegger imaginable. When it comes to the philosopher's fourfold of earth, sky, gods, and mortals, Norberg-Schulz interprets the first two as meaning the *actual* earth beneath our feet and sky above our heads, which is not at all what the Heideggerian fourfold is about.[35] So much the better, for without this mistake, we would have lost the author's sensitive accounts of the differing relations between earth and sky in the Nordic forest and the Arabian desert. The first of these landscapes encourages belief in elves, trolls, and other mythical creatures who inhabit the countless niche microclimates of forested waterlands, while the second issues directly into the big-skied *tawhid* sublimity of Islam.[36] According to Norberg-Schulz, this leads to romantic architecture in the first case and what he calls "cosmic" architecture in the second. By contrast, the discrete yet visually accessible places of the Mediterranean world give rise to classical architecture, which is marked by sculptural rather than decorative form and a spirit of human energy.[37] In turn, these three styles give rise to such mixed movements as Gothic (romantic plus cosmic) and baroque (romantic plus cosmic plus classical).[38] Continuing his meditation on architecture and geography, Norberg-Schulz contends that while Ludwig Mies van der Rohe was a perfect fit for the spirit of Chicago, I. M. Pei's Hancock Tower ruined Copley Square in Boston outright.[39] Given that a city functions as a crossroads or gathering of forces from multiple locations, "the main historical cities are . . . hardly found in places where a particular natural character is revealed (such as Delphi or Olympia), but somewhere like Athens that lies *between* these places."[40] All these remarks stem from Norberg-Schulz's disciplinary insight rather than from his philosophical dabbling, but his basically Heideggerian standpoint becomes clear from any number of passages. Early on, he asks us not to miss "the concrete environmental character . . . the very quality which is the object of man's identification, and which may give him a sense of existential foothold."[41] Heidegger himself might easily have written that "to create a place means to express the essence of being."[42] Norberg-Schulz openly cites the philosopher before telling us that "the meaning of architectural concretization . . . [is] *to set a place into work,* in the sense of concrete building."[43] What ultimately links Heidegger and Norberg-Schulz is their shared emphasis on local rootedness over rationalist abstraction.

If we shift our focus from theory to architecture, the best example of "Heideggerian" architecture is no doubt the work of Peter Zumthor of Switzerland, winner of the 2009 Pritzker Prize. His enchanting Therme Vals baths are just the sort of playground for the senses that Pallasmaa

Peter Zumthor, Therme Vals baths, Switzerland. Creative Commons Attribution-Share Alike 3.0 Unported. Photograph by Kazunori Fujimoto.

and Norberg-Schulz seem to have in mind. When reading Zumthor's prose, what first strikes the reader is a dose of conservative caution. As a student, he reports, he and his friends were always looking for some revolutionary answer to every problem they faced: "Not until later did I realize that there are basically only a very few architectural problems for which a valid solution has not already been found."[44] It is not just that history becomes more important to humans as they age: more than this, "our times of change and transition do not permit big gestures."[45] The same words might have been spoken by a historical postmodernist such as Michael Graves or Robert Stern, but that is not Zumthor's approach. His basically phenomenological stance is clear in his writings as in his buildings. He notes that "sense emerges when

I succeed in bringing out the specific meanings of certain raw materials in my buildings," an insight he credits to the influential German artist Joseph Beuys.[46] Zumthor declares that he wants to create buildings that seem to be part of their surroundings, and that speak to the emotions no less than to the mind.[47] He aspires further to a sense of warmth in his buildings, crafting them into human refuges in a more than metaphorical sense: more than most architects, he expresses a special concern for the temperature of his rooms.[48] Despite this conscious tailoring of things to people, Zumthor keeps one eye fixed on the architectural things themselves. After citing a story by Italo Calvino, Zumthor salutes this author for his "implication that richness and multiplicity emanate from the things themselves if we observe them attentively and give them their due."[49] He is quite specific about this, going so far as to share some detailed techniques: "I take a certain amount of oak and a different amount of *pietra serena* and add something to them: three grams of silver or a handle that turns or maybe surfaces of gleaming glass, so that every combination of materials yields a unique composition, becomes an original."[50] Nor does he forget the kinetic aspect of architecture: "I like the idea of arranging the inner structures of my buildings in sequences of rooms that guide us, take us places, but also let us go and seduce us. Architecture is the art of space and it is the art of time as well—between order and freedom, between following a path and discovering a path of our own, wandering, strolling, being seduced."[51] At times he sounds almost like his polar opposite Peter Eisenman, insisting on the object as something self-contained. Yet far from excluding the human being from architecture, Zumthor proclaims that "the sensation of beauty is not ignited by the form itself but rather by the spark that jumps from it to me," a concept that closely approaches the OOO version of hybrid objects.[52]

Architectural phenomenology has its critics, many of them quite severe. Some of the criticisms are based in politics, aimed both at Heidegger's own Nazism and at the spirit of political indifference typical of other phenomenologists. Under the influence of Heidegger and Merleau-Ponty, the architects just mentioned manage to formulate thoughts of genuine relevance to building, and in many cases have succeeded in putting those thoughts into action. But what might be said about the weaknesses of architectural phenomenology? Michael Benedikt worries about architecture becoming swamped by what he calls "experientialism": "the belief that what gives a building value, aside from fulfilling its shelter functions, is how its views and spaces make us personally feel as we move around."[53] He proposes instead an ethical basis for architecture in something like Martin Buber's I-Thou relationship.[54] Eisenman, a very different sort of person from Benedikt, would insist that one must choose between phenomenology and formalism. As he sees it, the choice for phenomenology means plunging into an architecture focused on our relations with the world, thereby inscribing oneself in the same "humanist" tradition dominant from the Renaissance through historical postmodernism. While this argument is certainly memorable, it is too close to the sort of formalism defended by Kant and by the art historian Michael Fried in his early period, when he mistakenly held that getting rid of humans is the key to autonomy. In one phase of Eisenman's architectural work, this entails the active subversion of human convenience with deliberately misplaced columns and other obstructions. Yet there is nothing inherently tainted about the sounds, textures, and kinetic paths experienced by people in a building. As we will see, the worry that humans have the power to ruin architecture just by experiencing it amounts merely to humanism with a sad face rather than a smiley one.

Nonetheless, there is more than a grain of truth in Eisenman's critique of architectural phenomenology. The latter's exquisite attention to nuanced human experience risks limiting itself to what OOO calls the sensual realm, at the expense of the extrahuman real. In the end, there is more to reality than the experience of temperature, oak, silver, and softly turning handles. If Kant were with us today, he might criticize the phenomenologists for paying too much attention to what he calls "charm":

> In beautiful views of objects, taste seems to fasten not so much on what the imagination *apprehends* in that area, as on the occasion they provide for it to engage in *fiction*, i.e. on the actual fantasies with which the mind entertains itself as it is continuously being aroused by the diversity that strikes the eye. This is similar to what happens when we watch, say, the changing shapes of the flames in a fireplace or of a rippling brook: neither of these are beauties, but they still charm the imagination because they sustain its free play.[55]

What such imaginative charm misses is the depth dimension of all experience: that to which it merely alludes rather than having directly available through friendly natural materials. Somewhat ironically for a tradition that relies so heavily on Heidegger, architectural phenomenology offers plenty of dwelling and numerous existential footholds, but far less *Angst* than we get from walking through Eisenman's own disturbing Memorial to the Murdered Jews of Europe, or from much of Daniel Libeskind's work.

Jacques Derrida

Jacques Derrida entered architectural discussion in the 1980s, considerably later than his first wave of impact in philosophy and literary criticism. Nonetheless, he arrived with the same package that characterized his advent elsewhere: celebrity charisma and considerable originality, burdened by a writing style idiosyncratic to the point of tedium. The Swiss architect Bernard Tschumi was Derrida's initial point of contact with the field, which resulted eventually in the philosopher's article "Point de folie—Maintenant l'architecture."[56] This famous but frustrating piece engages with Tschumi's Parc de la Villette project in Paris in the usual Derridean manner of calling everything into question while playing on the triple or even quintuple meanings of key terms. It is my view, at least, that this article has not aged as well as Derrida's best work. Perhaps better known is his extensive engagement with Eisenman in *Chora L Works,* a book of many media: transcripts, essays, even physical holes punched straight through the paper.[57] Destined to be a collector's item, this volume does have significant historical value, though the reader is likely to find more satisfaction in other writings of Derrida— not to mention those of Eisenman and his coeditor Jeffrey Kipnis, both of them central figures in the meeting of architecture and deconstruction.

Another crucial figure for Derrida's entry into architecture is Mark Wigley, originally from New Zealand. Wigley's doctoral thesis on Derrida would later become the influential book *The Architecture of Deconstruction,* which is mercifully free of any effort to imitate the style of its model. While there is little about architecture per se in this book, Wigley makes up for it in his catalog essay for the legendary 1988 Deconstructivism show at the Museum of Modern Art in New York, which he cocurated with the elderly Philip Johnson.[58] Such was the stature of the participants, and the importance of the exhibition's theme, that it can probably be called the most recent canonical show in the discipline. Although the included architects vary in the degree to which the "Deconstructivist" label fits them, each of the chosen projects is a good match for the show's theme. The level of quality assembled by the curators only becomes more remarkable with the passage of time: even three decades later, we find that the show featured a plausible—though by no means conclusive—list of the most influential designers of the past thirty years. From oldest to youngest, they are as follows: Frank Gehry (born 1929), Eisenman (born 1932), Coop Himmelb(l)au (Wolf Prix, born 1942, and Helmut Swiczinsky, born 1944), Rem

Koolhaas (born 1944), Tschumi (born 1944), Libeskind (born 1946), and the late Zaha Hadid (1950–2016).

Philosophers are generally aware of the existence of Deconstructivist architecture, which in their minds is closely linked with Derridean deconstruction. And sure enough, cocurator Wigley must count as one of the major promoters of Derrida's fortunes in the architectural world. Nonetheless, when reading the catalog of the show, one is astonished to find that the French philosopher goes entirely unmentioned. The major referent, instead, is Russian Constructivism of the prerevolutionary and Leninist periods. Deconstructivism = deconstruction + Constructivism, after all, and the catalog chooses to emphasize internal disciplinary forces rather than ideas imported from philosophy. Johnson's foreword offers direct analogies between specific Deconstructivists and Constructivists, with Hadid styled as the new Vladimir Tatlin, while Gehry and Prix are linked with Aleksandr Rodchenko.[59] For his part, Wigley notes that in opposition to classical procedures, the Russian avant-garde used pure forms "to produce 'impure,' skewed, geometric composition . . . [and] an unstable, restless geometry."[60] The result was "a nest of competing and conflicting axes and forms."[61] For instance, in Tatlin's proposed 1919 Monument to the Third International, "pure geometric forms become trapped in a twisted frame, [seeming] to announce a revolution in architecture."[62] Wigley distinguishes further between early and late phases of the Russian movement. Already, even "the early work was not concerned with destabilizing structure. On the contrary, it was concerned with the fundamental purity of structure," though it combined pure forms in a way that "transformed dynamism into instability."[63] Yet the more the Russians became involved with exploring this instability, the more they felt the need to temper it. By the time the brothers Leonid, Victor, and Alexander Vesnin completed their design for a Palace of Labor in 1922–23, "the early [avant-garde] work [had] become merely an ornament attached to the roof of a classical composition of pure forms. The structure below remains undisturbed."[64] And with this, the original glimpse of instability was left behind: "The radical possibility was not . . . taken up. The wound in the tradition soon closed, leaving but a faint scar." That brings us to the dramatic role envisioned for the Deconstructivist projects of 1988. For as Wigley dramatically puts it: "These projects reopen the wound."[65]

In Russian avant-garde circles one name for the wound in question was "defamiliarization," introduced by the formalist literary critic Viktor Shklovsky, who has recently regained prominence among Anglophone readers.[66] This idea of defamiliarization has points in common with OOO's "deliteralization," though we should caution that the familiar and the literal can be stripped away only to a limited degree if the final effect is to be credible. This point was noticed as early as Aristotle, an underrated champion of metaphorical language who nonetheless cautioned against its excessive use. If too many normal words in a literal statement are replaced by unusual ones, he warns in the *Poetics*, the result will be a mere riddle. For instance, "I saw a man glue bronze on a man with fire" would be a needlessly puzzling way to refer to the typical Greek medical procedure of drawing blood through an incision.[67] A certain amount of reassuring mental ballast in any situation helps make the defamiliarized portions more believable. In any case, Wigley stresses the openly defamiliarizing aspect of the projects in his show. As he tells us:

> What makes them disturbing is the way they find the unfamiliar already hidden within the familiar context. . . . In one project, towers are turned over on their sides, while in others, bridges are tilted up to become towers, underground elements erupt from the earth and float above the surface, or commonplace materials become suddenly exotic.[68]

Now, Derrida's name is mentioned nowhere in Wigley's catalog essay. In a sense it hardly matters, since we know of Wigley's preoccupation with the philosopher, and the lexicographical resonance between deconstruction and Deconstructivism is obvious enough. But in another sense, the absence of Derrida from the most high-profile piece of writing in Wigley's career sheds light on something else: the fact that Deconstructivism links up not just with Derrida but with Heidegger and Deleuze as well. Consider Wigley's perfectly accurate statement that each of the 1988 Deconstructivist projects "assumes an uncanny presence, alien to the context from which it derives, strange yet familiar—a kind of sleeping monster which awakens in the midst of the everyday."[69] But to speak of "the uncanny" is to invoke *das Unheimliche,* a term of Heideggerian rather than Derridean origin.[70] As mentioned, there may not be a more *unheimlich* experience in architecture than walking through Eisenman's menacing field of cubes in central Berlin, yet this is more a Heideggerian stroll than a Derridean one, despite Eisenman's closer identification with the latter philosopher. Moving in the other direction, Libeskind's signature work, the 2001 Jewish Museum in Berlin, has more of a disjointed Derridean feel to it than an *Angst*-ridden Heideggerian one, even though Libeskind is on record as having been more influenced by Heidegger, and though other architectural observers tend to affirm this self-assessment.[71] The point of these remarks is that any precaution about overidentifying Deconstructivism with Derrida is motivated not just by the important role also played by Russian Constructivism. Beyond this architectural point, Derrida is by no means the sole *philosophical* influence on the 1988 show, which points not only backward to Heidegger but also forward to Deleuze, whose influence on building would not become palpable until five years later. Consider the following remark by Wigley: "There are no simple windows, no regular openings puncturing a solid wall; rather, the wall is tormented—split and folded."[72] The idea of the fold would soon be Deleuze's signature contribution to architecture, even if the phrase "no simple windows" has a more Derridean flavor.

Daniel Libeskind, model of the Jewish Museum, Berlin. Creative Commons Attribution 2.0 Generic. Photograph by Naotake Murayama.

Speaking of Derrida, we should note that his *subverbal* presence in Wigley's catalog essay is unmistakable. Attempting another approach to the projects in his show, Wigley explains that they "twist Constructivism. This twist is the 'de' of 'de-constructivist.' The projects can be called deconstructivist because they draw from Constructivism and yet constitute a radical deviation from it."[73] In her highly critical review at the time, Catherine Ingraham complained that "the style of the catalog and the exhibition wanders aimlessly between a loose form of constructivism and a loose form of poststructural theory as if it were trying to conceal the tensions between these two positions."[74] Such concealment is noticeable, though I for one read it less as a suppression of discord than as an effort to ground the show's precedents exclusively in the Russian avant-garde while airbrushing Derrida from the picture—which may reflect the wishes of the older Johnson. Even so, Wigley's own fascination with Derrida resurfaces in indirect form. What is new in Deconstructivism, he tells us, is that irregular geometry "is no longer produced simply by the conflict between pure forms. It is now produced *within* those forms."[75] This is better, he reports, than merely distorting the form from outside, since this would only "[produce] a decorative effect, an aesthetic of danger, an almost picturesque representation of peril—but not a tangible threat."[76] But as soon as distortion and irregularity are placed *inside* the forms, we have left the atmosphere of the great Russian projects and enlisted in a full-blown Derridean assault on the classical law of identity. This becomes clear in some further passages by Wigley that might have come straight from the philosopher's desk: "This is an architecture of disruption, dislocation, deflection, deviation, and distortion, rather than one of demolition, dismantling, decay, decomposition, or disintegration. It displaces structure instead of destroying it."[77] Or in this passage even more: "It becomes unclear which came first, the form or the distortion, the host or the parasite. . . . To remove the parasite would be to kill the host."[78] And finally: "A deconstructive architect is therefore . . . one who locates the inherent dilemmas within buildings."[79] The same holds for Wigley's general description of the show as one in which "form is contaminated."[80] One might claim, of course, that "architects already knew" before Derrida that pure forms can contaminate each other, and that form can be disrupted, dislocated, deflected, deviated, distorted, and the like. But the problem with saying so is that Wigley tries to establish the novelty of the 1988 architects against their Russian forerunners by noting that contamination has shifted, from the point where pure forms meet into the heart of form itself. Since no architectural precedent is cited for this further step, we sense that the unspoken precedent for Deconstructivist innovation is Derrida himself.

Before moving on, we should note what Wigley's essay has to say about the role of function in Deconstructivism. In his view, the Russians ultimately turned their back on instability because they were "corrupted by the purity of the Modern movement," which famously stripped away ornament in the name of a smooth and streamlined aesthetic.[81] Despite the functionalist reputation of the modernists, they were actually "obsessed by an elegant *aesthetic* of functionalism, not by the complex dynamics of function itself."[82] Indeed, Wigley makes a good case that Deconstructivism has a more realistic sense of the intricacies of function than does modernism itself: "The modernists argued that form follows function, and that functionally efficient forms necessarily had a pure geometry. But their streamlined aesthetic disregarded the untidy reality of actual functional requirements."[83] This leads him to the daring motto that for the Deconstructivists, "instead of form following function, function follows deformation."[84] Furthermore, since this style entails discontinuity, it also demands a *break* between a building and its surrounding context. We can only salute Wigley's remark that "contextualism has been used as an excuse for mediocrity, for dumb servility to the familiar."[85] Yet he takes this too much in a Kantian or Friedian direction that is quick to jettison any human ingredient in architecture. For as Wigley puts it, and as Eisenman would also put it: "The object becomes the site of all theoretical inquiry."[86] While this might sound rather OOOish at first, it should be remembered that object-oriented ontology does not conceive of the object as that which is left once humans are subtracted from the picture. For OOO, the term "object" refers not just to inanimate things but also to humans, as well as to hybrids containing both human and nonhuman elements. There are countless examples of the latter. For instance, the Los Angeles Police Department does not become more truly an object if we fire all its officers, and neither would architecture become more real in a postapocalyptic landscape following human extinction. The object is only "the site of all theoretical inquiry" if we remember that humans are just another object among others, even if one with special and fascinating powers.

Near the end of Wigley's essay we find a prophetic passage: "The episode [of the 1988 Deconstructivism show] will be short-lived. The architects will proceed in different directions. . . . This is not a new style."[87] No indeed. More than thirty years later, it would be strange to think of Eisenman and Koolhaas as architectural allies, or Hadid and her former teacher Tschumi, or to imagine Gehry partnering with Libeskind and Prix. Even so, Johnson and Wigley managed to assemble a number of important figures who will all have some place in architectural history, and they did so through a convincing shared idea: unstable form distorted from within. Kipnis even suggests that the projects *had* to be framed as idiosyncratic one-offs rather than exemplars of a new style, given the strictures against novelty at the time from both the postmodern right and the politicized left: "The discipline of architecture has recognized them as exotic, precisely so as to suppress their contribution to a new architecture."[88] In any case, the 1988 Deconstructivism show at MoMA is one of those landmarks, found in every field, that allow us to gauge how much movement has occurred since we passed it.

Gilles Deleuze

The Deconstructivism show was not the only thing going on in 1988. In the same year, an aging Deleuze published his book *The Fold*, which a few years later (especially following English translation in 1992) would suggests a very different direction for architects. Two other people should be mentioned immediately in connection with Deleuze. One is the psychiatrist Félix Guattari, Deleuze's coauthor on four influential books, most notably *Anti-Oedipus* and its sequel, *A Thousand Plateaus.* The other is Gilbert Simondon, who worked in close intellectual proximity to Deleuze as a thinker of genesis and individuation. Simondon's most important writings were long blocked from English translation for family and legal reasons, but are just now becoming available, offering a possible second flowering for theorists of a Deleuzian stripe.[89] Even so, our focus here will be on Deleuze himself. Some years ago I attended a lecture by a respected dean of architecture who tried to explain the influence of various philosophers on the discipline. His first slide paired Heidegger with Norberg-Schulz, a familiar phenomenological duo. His second placed Derrida alongside Wigley's *The Architecture of Deconstruction,* another fitting selection. In his third slide, Deleuze was humorously matched with "any book with a foreword by Sanford Kwinter." It was a joke that struck the mark, given Kwinter's enduring status as a kind of Deleuzian ambassador to architecture, a field where he has long been an influential critic.

Since this book will be closely concerned with the status of formalism in architecture, let's turn straightaway to Kwinter's thoughts on the topic. His major interest, like that of most authors working in a Deleuzian idiom, is that form be reconceived in dynamic rather than static terms. The static approach, he claims, is the result of a "sloppy conflation" of the two very different notions of form and object.[90] Instead of being object-oriented, discussions of form should focus on its emergence from a prior resonant field. "What I call true formalism," Kwinter writes, "refers to any method that diagrams the proliferation of fundamental resonances and demonstrates how these accumulate into figures of order and shape."[91] His emphasis on the dynamic over the static is also connected with his opposition to manifest form in favor of something less tangible: "The manifest form—that which appears—is the result of a computational interaction between internal rules and external (morphogenetic) pressures that, themselves, originate in other adjacent forms (ecology)."[92] These ideas smell like Simondon even more than like Deleuze, though there is nothing here with which Deleuze would disagree. The primary philosophical interest of Simondon is that individual entities be treated according to their *process of individuation* rather than as fully formed individuals, a view that in some respects harks back to the pre-Socratic philosophers of the formless, blob-like *apeiron.* Simondon's primary target is Aristotle, whom he habitually accuses of a "hylomorphism" in which static forms take up residence in shapeless matter, thereby neglecting the meta-stable dynamism already found in matter itself. This cele-bration of dynamic matter ultimately leads us back beyond Henri Bergson and Baruch Spinoza—both favorites of Deleuze and his circle—to the works of that martyr of phi-losophy Giordano Bruno, burned at the stake in 1600.[93] All of this makes a perfect fit with the general antisubstance tendencies of recent philosophy, through which becoming is preferred to being and verbs can do no wrong, with nouns and substances confined to an everlasting penalty box.[94]

For Kwinter as for most Deleuzians, special stress must be laid on the concept of "the event." One of the problems faced by thinkers working in this tradition is that they end up hav-ing to emphasize novelty twice, since the first kind of event is too broad to account for the second. That is to say, they begin by upholding the Bergsonian model of a constant flow of creative novelty in every tiniest corner of the universe; everything is continuous change, with nothing remaining the same for even the least part of an instant. Or rather, there is not even such a thing as a single instant, due to the utterly orgasmic level of flux found at the heart of all things. But then, as if suddenly realizing that this makes novelty so easy to come by that there is little room left for truly remarkable change, they superadd a novelty that is somehow even more novel than just the regular sort. So it is with the term "event." Kwinter himself links events with the mathematical notion of *singularities,* "referring to those critical points or moments within a system when its qualities and not just quantities undergo a fundamental change."[95] A similar vein in Deleuze is mined by Manuel DeLanda, Kwinter's fellow New Yorker, and also a veteran teacher at architecture schools.[96] Kwinter writes nicely, just as DeLanda would, about the multiple singularities found by a climber in an ostensibly featureless rock wall.[97] He also brings us into the vicinity of "catastrophe theory" mathematician René Thom, another favorite of many who work on Deleuze and architecture.[98]

Turning for a moment to DeLanda, there is at least one important way in which he differs from Kwinter. Although both authors are fascinated by singularities, attractors, and disembodied topologies, Kwinter is the more markedly hostile to individual entities, and for this reason more hostile to OOO. According to his own reconception of time and dynamics, he announces, "the unitariness of the object would necessarily vanish."[99] Yet the subjunctive mood is misleading, since he treats this result as a *fait accompli*:

> What comes to the fore are, on the one hand, those relations that are smaller than the object, that saturate it and compose it, the "micro-architectures" for lack of a happier term, and on the other, those relations or systems that are greater or more extensive than the object, that comprehend or envelop it, those "macro-architectures" of which the "object," or the level of organization corresponding to the object, is but a relay member or part.[100]

The "micro-" and "macro-" terminology helps highlight the difference with DeLanda, who openly rejects what he calls "micro-reductionism" and "macro-reductionism"—the equivalent of OOO's undermining and overmining—as forms of unchecked analysis that efface what they were meant to explain in the first place.[101] Stated more directly, Kwinter is the advocate of a duomining analysis—a combination of undermining and overmining—that tries to replace any entity with both its components and its effects: a game of hot potato in which we must always move either downward or upward from any given point, and from there to some other point, until it turns out that no potato exists anywhere in particular. More often than not, Kwinter prefers the overmining to the undermining direction. This can be seen when he downplays objects in favor of "what I am calling 'practices'—[which] correspond less to formed and distinct objects than to *a specific regime* (of power, of effects) that for a given time inhabits the social field."[102] With the "social field" proposed as the ultimate arbiter of reality, the upward side of the reduction is clearly dominant. This is a point where we observe Kwinter veering sharply toward the ideas of Michel Foucault.[103]

Also relevant here is Stan Allen's work on field conditions. In a widely read 1997 article from *Architectural Design*, he shares his "intuition of a shift from *object* to *field* in recent theoretical and visual practices."[104] In this spirit, Allen encourages us to "think of the figure not as a demarcated object but as an effect emerging from the field itself—as moments of intensity, as peaks or valleys within a continuous field."[105] Pushing his understated Gestalt analogy further, he declares that "if classical composition sought to maintain clear relations of *figure on ground,* which modern composition perturbed by the introduction of a complicated play of *figure against figure,* with digital technologies we now have to come to terms with the implications of a *field-to-field* relation."[106] Much like Kwinter, Allen assumes that reducing the role of the figure means reducing the role of the object as well; an object cannot be a ground, for the simple reason that it cannot be a field. This resonates with Deleuze's own suspicion toward discrete individual entities, given the need for his "virtual" to be a continuum, despite his repeated insistence that this continuum also happens to be heterogeneous. A similar problem haunts Heidegger as well. Being is not only hidden as opposed to present, but is also implicitly taken to be unified, by contrast with the manyness of mere beings present before us.

In any case, Allen's concern with removing the figure/

ground relation in favor of a complexity embedded in the world's immanent surface can be found in nearly all writers concerned with Deleuze. John Rajchman, for instance, finds fault with Venturi for reducing "complexity to a given totality and simplicity of compositional elements," and with Colin Rowe for reducing "depth to the simultaneity of figure and ground." In a Deleuzian spirit, Rajchman prefers to look "along the surfaces, in their intervals and midsts for what may yet happen, coming thus to see that 'the most profound is the skin.'"[107] For Allen's part, he too gives practical architectural reasons for advocating fields over objects. Writing in the 1990s, he notes that the architectural theory of the time is torn between postmodern historical contextualism and Deconstructivism's "forceful rejection of context."[108] He gives a memorable description of the Umayyad mosque in Córdoba, Spain ("an undifferentiated but highly charged field") by contrast with St. Peter's in Rome ("elaborating and extending a basic geometric schema").[109] Yet here, as with Kwinter, the abandonment of figures in favor of fields is an extreme solution to an inherently less extreme problem. After all, Allen's desire for "permeable boundaries, flexible internal connections, multiple pathways and fluid hierarchies" can also be satisfied by a theory that does not dissolve individuals altogether into a field of local intensities.[110]

We come at last to the precocious designer Greg Lynn. Although Kwinter and then Kipnis were two of the earliest architectural theorists to signal the discipline's shift from Derrida to Deleuze, one could say that Lynn's pro-Deleuzian statement of 1993 marked a ceremonial end to the Derridean era in the field. Hadid was the youngest architect featured in the 1988 Deconstructivism show, but Lynn was a full generation younger. In fact, he was not yet thirty years old when he assisted the countermovement to Deconstructivism with his essay "Folding in Architecture." Here Lynn openly admires the turn to architectural complexity undertaken in the 1960s with Venturi's landmark book. What he doubts are the specific Venturian and Deconstructivist methods of designing complexity. Looking back in 2003 on his writings of a decade earlier, Lynn recalls that his motive at the time was "to move beyond Venturi's pictorial collage aesthetics and the formal and spatial collage aesthetics that then constituted the vanguard of complexity in architecture, as epitomized by Johnson and Wigley's . . . exhibition at MoMA in 1988."[111] As he had stated in 1993, "Neither the reactionary call for unity [by historical postmodernism] nor the avant-garde dismantling of it seems adequate as a model for contemporary architecture and urbanism."[112] Lynn dreamed instead of an architecture of "voluptuous forms" and "intricate assemblages," and whatever the merits of Deconstructivism, it cannot satisfy those particular wants. The Deleuzian path was Lynn's way out of what he viewed as the architectural impasse following 1988, though he also tips his hat to parallel trends inspired by Thom's catastrophe theory and the complexity theory of Stuart Kauffman and his associates.[113]

It is also worth noting that the young Lynn shows some ambivalence toward the established older stars of his profession. We have seen that he links the Deconstructivists with Venturi's already aging vision of complexity. As he put it in 1993: "The most paradigmatic architecture of the last ten years, including Robert Venturi's Sainsbury Wing of the National Gallery [in London], Peter Eisenman's Wexner Center [at Ohio State University], Bernard Tschumi's La Villette park [in Paris] or the Gehry House [in Santa Monica, California], invests in the architectural representation of contradictions."[114] Here the reader half expects Lynn to throw down the gauntlet and announce a generational break with these figures. But just two pages later, he suggests that once we take a closer look at some of these projects, they turn out to be his unwitting allies. For instance: "Rather than valorize the conflicts the [Gehry] house engenders . . . a less contradictory and more pliant logic would identify, not the degree of violation, but the degree to which new connections were being exploited."[115] Likewise, Eisenman's Wexner Center might seem at first glance like a textbook piece of Deconstructivism, and "is conventionally portrayed as a collision of . . . conflicting geometries." But even so, "Eisenman's project has [also] suggested recessive readings of continuous non-linear connection." In sum, "within the continuities of Deconstructivism there are inevitable unforeseen moments of cohesion."[116] It is debatable whether such continuities are really to be found in the projects mentioned. But in any case, what Lynn prefers as his personal escape route from historical and Deconstructivist strategies is "an alternative smoothness."[117] Deftly deploying analogies from the kitchen, Lynn argues for a "folded mixture" that would be "neither homogeneous, like whipped cream, nor fragmented, like chopped nuts, but smooth and heterogeneous."[118] Along with this typically Deleuzian appeal to the "heterogeneous yet continuous," Lynn sets down other conditions that his alternative strategy ought to meet. One of them is "intricacy," which precludes both an overly continuous aesthetic and a soporific bond of form to functional obligation.[119] Lynn is also more interested in relation than in autonomy: the quasi-individual elements of his smooth architectural continuum not only lie midway between whipped cream and chopped nuts but are also "free intensities [that] become intricated by an *external force* exerted upon them jointly."[120] He expands on this point as follows: "Intensive organizations continually invite external influences within their internal limits so that they might extend their influence through the affiliations they make."[121] Here Lynn seems to concede Immanuel Kant's point that architecture is inherently relational, but he treats this as cause for celebration rather than shame.

But for Lynn, perhaps the most important architectural virtue is *movement*, the dominant concept in his 1999 book *Animate Form.* Here Lynn not only joins Bergson in opposing the model of time as a series of cinematic frames but

Peter Eisenman, Wexner Center for the Arts, Ohio State University, Columbus. Creative Commons Attribution-Share Alike International license. Photograph by RightCowLeftCoast.

also openly calls for forms that evolve. In this way, he wages half-declared war on the "ethic of stasis" that in his view follows from an excessive commitment to purity and autonomy.[122] Even Deleuze's beloved baroque era fails, Lynn holds, through its overemphasis on temporal points or stances.[123] Though technology is not yet capable of producing buildings that move in the literal sense of the term, Lynn suggests "a paradigm of motion and time that renders substance virtually animated and actually stable." This much is already possible, given that "rhythmic motion is manifest in stable-oriented form rather than in literally moving objects."[124] To this end, we need only "[supplant] the traditional tools of exactitude and stasis with gradients, flexible envelopes, temporal flows and forces."[125] The result of all this is what surely amounts to the best known of Lynn's architectural forms: the blob.[126] He argues that far from being mere amorphous masses, "blob assemblages are neither multiple nor single, neither internally contradictory nor unified. Their complexity involves the fusion of multiple elements into an assemblage that behaves as a singularity while remaining irreducible to any single simple organization."[127] He argues further that unlike more regular forms such as spheres, the blob is defined by its thoroughly relational way of being: "Unlike a conventional geometrical primitive such as a sphere, which has its own autonomous organization, a meta-ball [i.e., a blob] is defined in relation to other objects. Its center, surface area, mass, and organization are defined by other fields of influence."[128] Lynn clearly has sufficient command of his discipline to design forms without reference to authors in other fields, if that were his wish. Yet here again we find that active and intelligent people in any field are among the least likely to ignore valuable ideas coming from elsewhere. Lynn did his time with Deleuze, but he digested the concepts of the French philosopher in his own way and managed to justify them on plausible architectural grounds.

By the same token, Lynn was aware of the danger of an overly literal adaptation of these new ideas to architecture. In 1999 he expresses the worry that "[Deleuze's] *Le Pli* undoubtedly risks being translated into architecture as mere folded figures. In architecture, folded forms risk quickly becoming a sign for catastrophe."[129] This can be read as another half-veiled critique of the 1988 show, and we saw that Wigley's catalog essay had already tried to appropriate the idea of folds for the Deconstructivist idiom. But though Lynn warns in advance of the excessive use of folded shapes, he also denies that this is the only way to make use of

Deleuze for architectural purposes. The mistake is to assume that any contact made by architecture with other disciplines can only result in hopelessly literal adaptation. Such a fear would inevitably lead to a puritanical model of independent professions avoiding each other in a kind of phobic monasticism. No doubt Lynn already knew about smoothness as a possible design form before reading Deleuze, and we have seen that he was motivated in part by factors professionally irrelevant to Deleuze himself, such as the objections lodged against high modernist architecture from the mid-1960s onward and a certain fatigue with Venturi's brand of complexity. But architecture is not just a matter of guild technical tricks beyond the concern of untrained outsiders. It is also a tacit statement about the nature of reality, and this is where it crosses paths with philosophy. Architects may learn from philosophers, but they can also push back, as when Eisenman retorts to Derrida that his perpetual hedging about the exact meaning of *chora* and the subtleties of his critique of presence are of little use to the architect, who is asked to make something that will not collapse and kill its occupants.[130] But when Deleuze proposes that reality is basically continuous rather than discontinuous, it is hard to see why Allen or Lynn should be forbidden to entertain such a thesis—and explore its architectural consequences—simply because Deleuze himself was not a licensed designer of buildings.

Even so, insofar as architectural Deleuzians are making a statement about the nature of reality, I do have some disagreements with them. For one thing, I do not find Deleuze's discussion of Leibniz in *The Fold* to be a convincing interpretation of the German philosopher. As Lynn observes, Deleuze himself is basically a philosopher of smoothness or continuity. This means that when he approaches a thinker of discrete individuals like Leibniz, he can only deploy one of his famous "sodomite" interpretations, as he explains in the following well-known passage: "I saw myself as taking an author from behind and giving him a child that would be his own, yet monstrous."[131] In this very spirit, Deleuze's continuist Leibniz is a scandalous reversal of the main tendency of Leibnizian philosophy. Despite his role as the coinventor of calculus, Leibniz is not really a philosopher of the continuous at all, but one of the major figures in the philosophy of individual substance, a tradition whose historical backbone runs along the axis Aristotle–Aquinas–Leibniz, and which is cultivated actively today by OOO. Although the philosophical prestige of substance is currently as low as it has ever been, we must not lose sight of its remarkable innovations, which—among other things—will prove highly relevant to this book. Aristotle shifted our attention from otherworldly perfect forms to concrete individual entities here on earth. He was also the first Western philosopher to say that the root of philosophy—individual things, in his case—is destructible rather than eternal, something never permitted by the pre-Socratics or Plato. Aristotelian primary substance is able to endure changes in accidents, qualities, and relations without becoming something entirely different, thereby giving objects remarkable flexibility in entering different situations and absorbing and resisting various influences.

If we now skip forward to Leibniz, his great innovation was the idea that substance has an interior. Since no monad can make direct contact with any other, its interaction with other beings is somewhat like a movie playing in a theater no other monad can enter. Though I think I am observing the outer world directly, I am simply viewing a simulacrum that—thanks to God's decree of preestablished harmony—happens to correspond to a reality I can never directly touch. Like all traditions, the philosophy of substance has its downside as well: its granting of excessive priority to the natural over the artificial, its relative difficulty in dealing with hybrids and compounds, and—at least in Leibniz's hands—its regressive tendency to make substance indestructible again. Yet we cannot do justice to the insights of this tradition if we assume that the discrete is merely a surface effect of a deeper continuum—which is exactly what Deleuze tends to do, despite his claim to allow for both the heterogeneous and the continuous.[132] Since Leibniz's tiny monads have no windows, it makes little sense to think of him as a philosopher of relations; after all, no monad can relate to anything except by way of God. Aristotle already makes broad allowance for continua in his philosophy, especially in the *Physics*, where time, space, quantity, and change are all treated as continuous rather than as composed of ultimate units. But then there is the *Metaphysics*, in which there is always a definite number of substances in any given room; stated differently, substances are heterogeneous but by no means continuous. If architecture forgets this lesson, it will be left with no principle for positioning apertures or articulating façades and series of rooms. More than this, it might even lose its sense of the discrete and limited nature of any particular project. In this way it could misread urban space as a system of communication, rather than as a thick and noisy forest where communication is also obstructed and dampened.[133]

Basic Principles of the Book

By no means are these the only philosophers who have shaped recent architectural thinking. I have already alluded to Bruno Latour, whose network-based model is as intriguing to architects as it is to most everyone else. Yet so far there is no discernible Latourian design trend in the way that there is with Heidegger, Derrida, and Deleuze. The same holds for the German philosopher Peter Sloterdijk, whose massive *Spheres* trilogy has implications for our understanding of space, though here too we have not yet seen a full-fledged school of Sloterdijkian architecture, despite a recent growth of interest in his work.[134] Another figure that comes to mind is Luce Irigaray, as explored in the writings of Peg

Rawes.[135] And we can hardly omit one of the most influential thinkers of the past forty years: Foucault, whose ideas about disciplinary society have permeated two generations of human thought, architecture not excluded.[136]

Even so, it is safe to say that Heidegger, Derrida, and Deleuze are the three philosophers whose ideas have left the deepest imprints on actual design strategies in recent decades. Each of these currents has its own strengths and weaknesses. Heidegger and the phenomenological tradition have had important influence in ensuring that sensual experience is taken seriously, against various intellectualist attempts to dismiss such experience as "humanist." Since buildings are not just concepts, it is important to remember that they are expressed as surfaces glimmering with visual and tactile qualities. The downside here is excessive focus on the existentially grounded individual human, toasty warm in its ontological homeland, free of the ontic distractions of political strife. In addition, Heidegger's philosophy has a marked tendency to identify Being with the one and beings with the many, which wrongly suggests that the deep background of all experience is a monolithic lump devoid of internal complexity. As a result, the diversity of sensual experience in phenomenological architecture is sometimes haunted by a trace of superficiality, occasionally leading to melodramatic works that might well serve as stagings for Richard Wagner's *Ring* cycle. Granted, there is an impressive degree of craft that goes into much phenomenological work. Yet the fact remains that too much focus on human experience at the expense of the things themselves will always run the risk of histrionics.

Deconstructivist architecture easily avoids what is worst in Derrida: his wordiness, his lack of comfort in getting to the point. Architectural work in this vein is often genuinely disturbing, and frequently succeeds in shattering the literalist banalities of context. Deconstructivism's instinct for decomposition avoids the tacit holism of phenomenology, while

tempering Derrida's excessive love of nonidentity with architectural fact: a beam or column really just is itself, not everything else as well. Wigley is also right that Deconstructivism
is more honest about the intricate complexities of function
than high modernism, with its ultrastreamlined glass-and-
steel aesthetic trumping actual intricacy of function. On
the downside, Deconstructivism often shares Duchamp's
weakness for subversive and showboating pranks. Alongside the many impressive works in this vein, there are at
least as many moustaches on Mona Lisas, and they are never
funny twice. We should recall the aforementioned point that
defamiliarization works best when carefully positioned in a
broader zone of comfort, security, and predictability. Just as
every statement should not be a metaphor (to avoid riddles),
every statement should not be a joke (to avoid buffoonery).
Nor should a city consist primarily of existential crises. All
these factors suggest that this trend was always best suited
for one-off black-sheep monuments; it is safe to assume
that a Deconstructivist school of urban planning was never
in the cards.

Of Deleuzian architecture, as of the philosopher's own
works, what is best is the liberating spirit of irreverence.
Instead of niggling games with formal languages, we are
immersed in strange affiliations and the conversion of things
into centaur-like others. Admirably suited to surfing continuous waves, this style undercuts all assumptions of how to
articulate a building—or anything else—into its natural elements. The whole takes precedence over the parts, and this
inversion lends a remarkable consistency to even the tiniest
components. On the downside, there is the same problem
here as with phenomenology, in the sense that the ultimate
depth of the world is taken to be one. The typical Deleuzian
motto that the virtual is both heterogeneous and continuous
is scarcely credible, sounding more like a childhood birth-
day wish than a hard-earned philosophical result. In this
way, the genuine conflict between the continuous and the

discrete—which haunts every field from quantum theory to evolutionary biology—is falsely disdained as a pseudoproblem. Deleuze's long-standing tendency to distort historical figures (such as Leibniz) into perverse projections of himself is mirrored architecturally in the inability to face up to bona fide problems of articulation. Rebellion against the linear and the segmented is prematurely identified with victory in all cases. Every possible tension—building and context, structure and envelope, mass and ornament—is too easily resolved before even getting under way.

The moment of OOO's arrival in the architectural world corresponds closely to a moment of growing fatigue with Deleuze, the most recent philosopher in the series. A group of architects of roughly my own age (I was born in 1968) began wrestling with topics that have a notably object-oriented feel, and through them I became involved in architectural discourse. Not everyone has been pleased by this development. Consider the following remark by Bryan Norwood in the pages of *Log*: "There is a tendency to set up the appeal to [OOO] as part of a move from thinking in terms of continuous flows (which has been associated with Deleuze) to thinking through discrete objects. . . . But the ontological evaluation that all objects withdraw is not yet a design theory."[137] Norwood is right that OOO has broad appeal to architects who have tired of the paradigm of continuous flows. He is also right that the phrase "all objects withdraw" is not enough to qualify as a design theory. The problem lies in what he gets wrong: OOO is not primarily a theory of hiddenness, but of the often tortuous relations between objects and their own qualities. Stated differently, OOO is a passionately *antiliteralist* theory, and the meaning of this phrase will prove to be one of the central topics of this book. But first, we should speak a bit more about architecture and its history.

2   I KNOW NOT WHAT

READERS OF PHILOSOPHY ARE AWARE THAT THE ANCIENT WRIT-
ings of this discipline have not survived in their entirety.
While this is especially true of the pre-Socratic thinkers,
from whom we mostly have fragments and citations by
others, important works are missing even from figures as
central as Aristotle. But the situation in architecture is even
more dire, since here only one ancient text has survived.
Vitruvius, a Roman architect and engineer in the employ of
Julius and then Augustus Caesar, authored his *Ten Books on
Architecture* sometime around 25 B.C. Although this work was
never entirely forgotten, and was referred to intermittently
from at least the Carolingian period forward, it was not a
strong influence on the Romanesque and then Gothic con-
structions that dominated medieval Europe.[1] Only during the
Renaissance, with its proverbial return to classical culture,
did Vitruvius attain the status of an ancient authority and
inspire other theoretical works of comparable magnitude.
Hence the strange result that the first great extant treatise on architecture was written before the birth of Christ,

while the second was not published until 1452: Leon Battista Alberti's *De re aedificatoria*.[2] A rough analogy would be if the two oldest works of philosophy in our possession were the *Enneads* of Plotinus and Descartes's *Meditations,* separated as they are by a comparable fourteen-century span. Yet since Alberti's time the pens of architects have not rested, and the post-Renaissance corpus of architectural theory is at least as voluminous and sophisticated as that of philosophy. Architects have not just built but have also written about what they built (or hoped to build), and many have done so brilliantly. It is a field packed with versatile intellects who tend to be passionate and opinionated, and frequently even competitive and judgmental. Architects are mentally omnivorous like few others, and some have the scent of bloodhounds for new trends in every field. To give just one example, the turn from Derrida to Deleuze in the 1990s took place in architecture several years before it happened in philosophy.

Architecture has also been unusually open to the thoughts of outsiders and amateurs. In 1753, the Abbé Marc-Antoine Laugier appeared from nowhere to become a major voice in French architectural theory, with his notion of the "primitive hut" achieving a foundational role comparable to the "state of nature" in political theory.[3] When John Ruskin published his influential *The Seven Lamps of Architecture* in 1849, he still knew surprisingly little about the field; the book has nonetheless entered the canon of the discipline, even if its moralizing approach is annoying to many. In recent decades, a number of important architectural theorists have entered the field through the merest of accidents. Generally speaking, the professional crew in architecture is somewhat more complicated than that in philosophy, which has come to consist almost entirely of university professors who write books. There are architects who only build, and others who both build and write. There are architects who hope to build, but end up—at least for many years—with portfolios of unactualized projects, often supplemented by far-reaching essays and articles that flourish in print. There are also full-time theorists and historians who have no professional qualifications to build in the first place.

One of the overriding facts of the discipline, which surprised me greatly as a newcomer, is the truly minuscule percentage of architecture that ever sees the light of day. The vast majority of buildings one sees in a city are not designed by architects but erected by construction companies in accordance with banal but efficient templates. High-profile building projects are often put up by large corporate firms located nowhere near the avant-garde of the profession, though some of these companies do a fine job of translating advanced ideas into publicly acceptable form. Major projects often hold open competitions that draw literally thousands of entries assembled on very short notice, and most of these go nowhere despite immense efforts by the hopeful. Jørn Utzon's winning design for the beloved Sydney Opera House was famously dug out of the discard pile by prominent jury member Eero Saarinen. Often enough, even the winner of a competition will find that the project is canceled at the last minute, or that severe modifications are demanded: Utzon's Sydney project was extensively altered by others and took years of cost overruns to complete, by which time the architect himself had already resigned in frustration. In this respect there is something of the pipe dream about much architectural work, and in cases of success the architect must also be skilled—in a way that most philosophers and artists simply are not—in navigating the spheres of finance, politics, and media in order to bring a project to completion. In one recent case, an acquaintance of mine expended less energy on his initial design than on outmaneuvering both a rival architect and a hostile mayor for the winning entry ever to begin construction. The story is not atypical. For a life that can be so glamorous and satisfying when it goes well, the practice of architecture is often littered with obstructions.[4]

This chapter will focus on two topics of particular relevance to my argument. The first is the architectural distinction between "form" and "function," already familiar to the educated public. Since these terms have been defined in various ways across the centuries, it will be useful to specify what I mean by them here. As will be explained in a later chapter, by "form" I mean the reality of a thing apart from any of the relations in which it engages. This obviously excludes most utilitarian function. But it also excludes the visual *look* of a thing—even though this is precisely what many people mean by aesthetic "form"—since this look is partly dependent on the beholder, and therefore belongs to the sensual realm of experience rather than to the reality of form in its own right. There is precedent for my usage in medieval philosophy's concept of the hidden "substantial form" in things, later abolished by suspicious moderns with their reflexive distrust of occult qualities and dormitive principles. By "function" I refer not just to the narrowly practical results of a thing but also to *any of its relations,* even if these might seem purely cosmetic or conceptual. For the purposes of this book it is therefore possible to replace the form/function pair with that of reality/relation; given the stylistic need for flexible synonyms to avoid tiresome repetition, I will use these pairs interchangeably. It is important to note that these terms are not meant in a taxonomical sense, as if certain aspects of a building must always fall on one side or the other. The hidden form of a thing can always be made partly accessible to relations, otherwise it would be unthinkable for an edifice to express its function in any way, and even impossible for forms to exist among other entities in the world. Conversely, a relational function can always be de-relationized (or "zeroed") by being treated as a self-contained unit.

Along with form and function, a second important architectural distinction is that between the use of established historical or rational principles on one side and the recourse to personal invention on the other. This point has usually arisen in questions pertaining to form, since innovations in function tend to come from outside architecture itself. The demand for airports or cybercommerce fulfillment centers was not decided by architects, though there may be classes of buildings for which architects anticipate a need before it is generally known. While the case for innovation initially centered on the freedom to "eyeball" changes to the classical proportions of Vitruvius, or to adopt certain appealing features of the Gothic style à la carte, the case for innovation eventually hinged on the impenetrability of form to rational principle. For obvious reasons, this relative obscurity of form makes a good fit with OOO and its specific brand of realism, which considers the real to be much too real to be translated into visible renderings without distortion. Historically, some of the key steps in this direction were taken in the 1600s and 1700s with such terms as "character," "the picturesque," "the sublime," and the good old *je ne sais quoi.*[5]

Two Flanks of Vitruvius

One of the surest signs of the importance of Vitruvius, as of major authors in every field, is his penchant for being attacked simultaneously for opposite reasons—much like Kant at the hands of the living French philosophers Bruno Latour and Quentin Meillassoux, as we will see.[6] Although there have been various complaints about Vitruvius over the centuries, they boil down to a single dispute that motivates perennial controversy. For this celebrated Roman author, symmetry is a crucial feature of building, and the proportions of the human body are also of central relevance. The classical Doric, Ionic, and Corinthian orders entail differing proportions of "masculine" and "feminine" traits, and each of these has its proper architectural uses. The human body is said to have a basically circular form when the arms and legs are extended and moved, as later made famous in Leonardo da Vinci's drawing of "Vitruvian Man," now found on the back of the Italian one-Euro coin. The criticisms of this symmetrical, proportional, and human-centered outlook come in just two basic kinds: (1) "Vitruvius is too haphazard in his discussion of proportions; he is not rational or mathematical enough"; (2) "Vitruvius creates a rigid straitjacket of proportions that suppresses the individual architect's freedom; he is too rational and mathematical." Let's consider examples of both attitudes.

"Vitruvius Is Not Rational Enough"

■ Alberti found Vitruvius to be deficient as a writer when contrasted with such classics of Latin style as Cicero. More important, Alberti shared the proverbial Platonism of so many Renaissance figures, and thus demanded a greater exactitude of balanced mathematical proportion in the various parts of a building. The term he used for this was *concinnitas* (roughly, "harmony"), which originally referred in Latin to a well-mixed drink.

■ Early modern French architecture, heavily classicist in outlook, liked to treat the beauty of form in terms of a pure mathematical grammar. Although Vitruvius and Alberti were key sources for this brand of classicism, French architectural thought tended to push matters further. This eventually led to the famous *querelle des anciens et des modernes* of the late 1600s, centered on François Blondel (not to be confused with his later namesake Jacques-François Blondel) and Claude Perrault, with Perrault defending the architect's freedom from rules and Blondel countering that this is permissible only in cases of rare individual genius.[7]

"Vitruvius Is Too Rational"

■ Others preferred the works of the moderns to those of the ancients, with the irony that "modern" initially referred to the medieval Gothic. The prominent mannerist architect Sebastiano Serlio noted that ancient Roman buildings did not always follow Vitruvian proportions anyway, so a certain leeway was already needed in employing those principles.[8] Later, the term "modern" would refer to Michelangelo and other baroque and mannerist architects who departed from accepted classical proportions as they saw fit. A remarkable anecdote from 1665 nicely captures the dispute between these classical and modern approaches: when Louis XIV summoned Gian Lorenzo Bernini from Rome to Paris to work on the new palatial design for the Louvre, the asymmetry of Bernini's plan was questioned by the young secretary to the Minister Colbert, leading to an offended outburst from the Italian "starchitect."[9]

■ British classical architecture, unrestrained by any official academy as in France, differed in at least two respects from hard-core French classicism. The first was its deference to the late Renaissance architect Andrea Palladio

as the major authority, perhaps for a combination of aesthetic and religious reasons, which thereby pushed the
heart of the canon forward in time.[10] The second was
the greater British tolerance for eclecticism: famously,
Sir Christopher Wren showed both Gothic and baroque
elements in his buildings despite his generally classical
spirit.

■ At the surprisingly early date of 1721, an important work
by the Austrian architect Johann Bernhard Fischer von
Erlach opened the discipline to a wide range of influences
from as far afield as China and India.[11] This was a distant omen of the historicism of the 1800s, as well as an
early blow to any restricted circuit of historical influence
or monocultural picture of rationality.

■ From the 1740s there emerged the theme of "character" in architecture, over and above its specific accidental properties. This began with Germain Boffrand
before eventually reaching its peak in the pivotal figure
Antoine-Chrysostome Quatremère de Quincy, a classicist
by inclination.[12] In British gardening theory, which was
under heavy Chinese influence from the late 1600s, concern for the overall spirit of a design beyond its tangible
properties took the form of a fondness for the "picturesque." This was linked with wider discussions of the
aesthetic *je ne sais quoi* (I know not what) that escapes
exact rational formulation. Along with the parallel influence of British empiricist philosophy, it would give rise to
an early form of aesthetic relativism.

As concerns the twin themes of the form/function relation
and the rationalist/nonrationalist dispute, I will defend the
following views: (1) Form and function are insufficiently distinct to deserve their status as the two great pillars of architecture, though not for the reasons that have usually been
suggested.[13] The real reason is that both are conceived in too
relational a way, and their supposed difference is grounded in

a purported—though nonexistent—gulf between perception and praxis as two radically different modes of being. This is the same mistake made in philosophy by Heidegger: as if the unconscious use of a hammer and the conscious perception or theorizing of it were so utterly different in kind as to mark a great ontological divide. (2) Reality simply cannot be rationalized, and it follows that architecture cannot be the slave of any fixed proportional or mathematical rules. Thus I will argue for the importance of the hidden, and to some degree even of the picturesque. This puts me in partial alliance with two key works of the 1960s: Robert Venturi's defense of complexity and contradiction, and Aldo Rossi's antifunctional account of monuments and urban typology.[14] Sigfried Giedion makes the following historical claim: "Throughout history there persist two distinct trends—the one toward the rational and the geometrical, the other toward the irrational and the organic: two different ways of dealing with or of mastering the environment."[15] A potential problem here is that the organic can itself be defined in functional terms.[16] But what Giedion is really after becomes clear from his other opposition: the rational versus the irrational—roughly equivalent to the mathematico-geometrical versus a more elusive conception of form. Given that the term "irrational" usually functions as an insult rather than as an illuminating description, I will use "nonrational" instead.

Form and Function

The educated public is familiar with the phrase "Form follows function," which has a good case to be called the core duality of modern architecture. Edward Robert De Zurko's *Origins of Functionalist Theory* shows that fragments of functionalist ideas can be found throughout the history of architecture. But it may have been the Venetian priest Carlo Lodoli in the 1740s (his ideas not published until nearly a century later) who first suggested that form and function are the sole central terms for architecture.[17] Once this claim was first aired, it was a small step to considering form and function primarily in terms of each other. Any link between these terms will tend to have an anticlassicist ring, since the pressures on form are thereby shifted away from previous historical or proportional motivations and are leveraged instead by the specific needs of the project at hand.

It should go without saying that the notion of form following function opposes frivolous academic ornament, as colorfully denounced by Adolf Loos in his 1910 lecture "Ornament and Crime." Following the belated publication of Lodoli's ideas in 1834, further rapid steps were taken in a functionalist direction. An important example is Karl Bötticher's 1840s distinction between a building's *Kernform* (core structural purpose) and its *Kunstform* (decorative properties).[18] The Austrian Eduard van der Nüll argued further that ornamental form should express structural purpose, before tragically taking his own life in 1868 after his brilliant Vienna Opera House was panned by early critics.[19] Although the influential Gottfried Semper opposed Bötticher's *Kernform/Kunstform* distinction with the idea that structure should be masked rather than emphasized, tectonic or structural concerns remained a particular preoccupation in the Germanophone world.[20] These tendencies would eventually give rise to the prominent early modernist circle led by Otto Wagner in 1890s Vienna, and shortly thereafter to the competing school of Hermann Muthesius in Berlin.[21] A related issue was the growing awareness throughout the 1800s that form follows *material*, with a number of European architects recognizing that the increased use of iron called for new forms of building. Among the relevant figures here are Léonce Reynaud in France (1834), Eduard Metzger in still-independent Bavaria (1845), and the obscure English theorist Edward Lacy Garbett (1850).[22]

"Form follows function" is a snappier version of the phrase "Form ever follows function" from an 1896 article by

Louis Sullivan, Wainwright Building, St. Louis, Missouri. Photograph by Paul Piaget for HABS, 1967.

the Chicago-based Louis Sullivan, an early master of sky-scrapers and the onetime mentor of Frank Lloyd Wright.[23] Credit for the motto is sometimes given instead to the mid-century American sculptor Horatio Greenough, a friend of Ralph Waldo Emerson, though Sullivan gave final verbal form to the principle.[24] Greenough's primary concern was that Americans should discover their own style of building distinct from the European, demonstrating once more how an apparently universal rational principle (functionality) can link up so easily with nationalist motives (American authenticity). Greenough and Sullivan's underlying idea is simple, even if its philosophical pedigree is intricate, and even though Sullivan was in fact a fine ornamentalist and theorist of ornament.[25] Although paintings and sculptures may have a specific function in society, it is peripheral to their reality, whereas architecture has a preeminently functional role. Works of visual art can always be moved into museums or contexts other than their originally intended ones; while much hand-wringing occurs when this happens, artworks are basically amenable to being encountered in isolation, and can even be at their best in such solitude. This is why Kant's demand for a decontextualized "pure" beauty for artworks is basically plausible even if one opposes it. When it comes to architecture, the situation is different. It may seem obvious that the *function* of a building should be derived from the design brief: the building is to serve as a hospital, a factory, a residence, or a school, and must be a clear structural embodiment of these needs. But when it comes to the *form* of a building, it is by no means clear that this should spring directly from its purpose; indeed, we are still in the midst of centuries of debate over this very point.

Under the influence of Vitruvius, many premodern architects worked in one of the classical orders, with new variants added as the discipline unfolded. When travel to Greece became easier for non-Ottoman citizens in the mid-1700s, there was a new movement proclaiming the "classic" Romans to be poor copies of the more original Greeks, though Giovanni Battista Piranesi soon fired back on behalf of Rome.[26] Benjamin Latrobe designed the Bank of Pennsylvania around 1800, and with its Greek revival style it looked like a Parthenon in downtown Philadelphia, a decision that had its critics from the outset. Readers whose first exposure to architecture came with Ayn Rand's popular novel *The Fountainhead,* featuring heroic modernist Howard Roark as its central character, will be prepared in advance to react with horror to historically referenced architecture of this kind. Yet there is no a priori reason why the use of precedent should always be awful: if you hate Latrobe's bank, you may nonetheless find yourself stirred by the neo-Greek U.S. Capitol, or perhaps by the austere Egyptian obelisk known as the Washington Monument. Others remained strong advocates of the structural lightness of Gothic and its flying buttresses—as in the 1925 Chicago Tribune Tower of John Mead Howells and Raymond Hood—a preference that would have appalled the great figures of the Renaissance. In any case, the question of how to relate to precedent always gives rise to turbulent dispute, as witnessed again in the postmodernist controversy of the late twentieth century.[27]

Most important, Sullivan's idea that "form ever follows function" marks a closure of each building into itself. Whereas Harold Bloom treats each literary work as a duel with earlier works, Sullivan's approach would in principle cut off each building from its predecessors, which sounds strangely like a *formalist* principle. But can Sullivan really count as a formalist in the Kantian sense of the term? In one sense clearly not, since—as we will see—in Kant's eyes no architect could possibly qualify as a creator of formalist purity; insofar as architecture always has uses, it is excluded a priori from the level of autonomy that Kant demands. Even so, one can well imagine that Kant would not be displeased by Sullivan's motto. After all, by linking form exclusively to function Sullivan at least repels other possible influences, such as historicist decoration or arbitrary guidelines as to mathematical proportion. If the Kantian superego could speak to us today, it might say something like this: "Although architecture can never be truly autonomous, Sullivan makes a good go of it. He does define form solely in terms of function, which wards off the agreeable, the conceptual, the historical, the merely decorative, and other possible contaminants of pure form. In short, he makes architecture as autonomous as it can possibly be despite its built-in handicap of usefulness. Not bad, not bad at all." Now, Sullivan was by no means ignorant of philosophy; his thinking drew heavily on the transcendentalist ideas of Emerson and his circle.[28] But insofar as Sullivan's functionalist maxim excludes so many purported impurities, it is perhaps best to read "Form follows function" as an important variation on Kantian aesthetics. From here, we need only add a few twists before finding ourselves in a different aesthetic space altogether. It would make little sense to call Sullivan an architectural formalist in the more recent sense, since this would entail active suppression of a building's functional role in a way he would never have attempted. But perhaps there are ways to aestheticize or autonomize function without suppressing it. We will return to this topic below.

As mentioned previously, Sullivan's formula was not entirely without precedent.[29] It had not escaped the notice of earlier architects that something like form and something else like function seem to be present in architecture as central but distinct concerns. Already for Vitruvius there are three essential considerations: *firmitas, utilitas,* and *venustas,* famously rendered in Sir Henry Wotton's 1624 English translation—with the first two reversed—as "commodity, firmness, and delight." Since "firmness" has largely become the domain of structural engineers, we more often find architects focusing on "commodity" and "delight," or function and form. Alberti's own distinction between "structure" and "lineaments" does much the same work.[30] When we

consider function in its own right, it has an obviously relational meaning, which is what made Kant suspicious of it.
A building apparently makes sense only in connection with
its stated purpose. The soaring vault of a cathedral suggests
the half-concealed presence of the godhead. An airport offers
convenient processing of passengers and the safe landing
and taxiing of aircraft, and cannot perform its tasks if it gets
too cute and obstructs the runway with ornaments or Doric
columns. What Kant seems to have missed is that "form"
also has a relational sense, given that paintings and buildings are designed to appeal to humans—with their specific
cognitive and sensory equipment—rather than to dogs, ants,
or supercomputers. Whether we treat the form of a building
as its visible configuration or as something more subtle, form
is tacitly regarded as form *in relation to us*, making it "heteronomous" rather than autonomous in Kantian terminology.
Indeed, it is difficult to imagine an architecture that would
not appear hopelessly heteronomous to Kant, although he
readily claims autonomy for visual art by distancing it from
personal factors and cognitive paraphrase.

Formalism in the arts is a special case of ontological closure. As such, it faces two different and opposite problems
that arise from the same root: the taxonomical assumption
that we can put relations in one place and nonrelational form
in the other, with no account of how one can change into the
other. For example, we will see that in the autopoietic biology of Humberto Maturana and Francisco Varela, a strict distinction is made between the system of a living cell and the
environment surrounding it, but at the hidden cost of sub-
suming all organelles inside the cell into a strictly relational
system.[31] In other words, the specific wall between the cell
and the outside world is the only wall allowed for by their
theory. Although literary formalism insists that a poem be
cut off from its sociopolitical and biographical surroundings,
the work's interior is treated as a relational fiesta in which
every word and comma gains its meaning from the rest, so

that autonomy ends the very minute we pass through the gates of the work.[32] In the visual arts, Clement Greenberg demands that pictorial content be related solely to the flat canvas background rather than having any meaning in its own right; at most, in the case of collage, he permits the flat background to become multiple backgrounds at once.[33] But despite this autonomy of the unified background, Greenberg's pictorial surface is again a holistic zone where the elements of content have no mutual independence.

As for the two problems that emerge from such taxonomy, they are as follows: (a) *Any pure closure of an object from its environment fails to account for how relations are possible, and sometimes even desirable.* If we join the later Fried in pairing artwork with beholder and Sullivan in matching function with form, then Kantian purity is already lost in both cases. Yet the result is not that everything mixes with everything else; instead, maybe three, four, five, eight, or ten pieces of the environment are brought into play for the artwork. Formalism cannot be an instant result of banning from art our least favorite spheres of reality, but emerges in the wake of various amplifications and cancellations. (b) *The various elements that compose autonomous form are also partly autonomous from each other.* Rather than being a seamless or systematic web of sleek subcomponents, any form or object consists of a loose unity of independent elements. Neglect of this second principle leaves Greenberg mute about the content of paintings and makes Heidegger openly contemptuous toward the merely "ontic" character of specific beings. On this note we turn to our second theme, which we might call the difference between the rational and the picturesque.

Je Ne Sais Quoi

The French phrase *je ne sais quoi* has long been used in everyday English to refer to a certain undefinable character in a person, place, or thing. Whatever it might refer to in any given case, the *je ne sais quoi* points beyond explicit statement and hints at a vague animating charisma in the thing that lies behind all its tangible traits. It is often used as a term of derision in modern philosophy, whose rationalist bias makes it suspicious of anything that cannot be transmitted cleanly in unambiguous propositional prose. In this context, accusations are frequently made of a "negative theology" that tells us only what something is not rather than what it is, as if any appeal to a *je ne sais quoi* were nothing but worthless hand-waving. The philosopher John Locke speaks of the substratum of all visible properties as an I-know-not-what. And while he plausibly adds that this unknown layer of things has much to do with their currently unexpressed *powers,* the reader senses a certain reluctance from Locke in affirming it at all, as if he would be happier if direct empirical access to everything were possible.[34] His successor in empiricist philosophy, George Berkeley, adds the radical novelty that no mystery exists beneath the palpable qualities of a thing; with Hume's skepticism, this aversion to the hidden and inapparent becomes a lasting inclination in Western philosophy.[35] Kant briefly revives the *je ne sais quoi* with his thing-in-itself, though his German Idealist heirs quickly abandoned it, even while retaining so much else from his thinking. In the twentieth century, Heidegger restored mysterious depth to partial favor with his discussion of Being as that which withdraws from all presence. It was also through Heidegger's influence that the *je ne sais quoi* regained entry into architectural theory, only to be flipped upside down once again, thanks to Derrida's suspicion of any "self-presence" of something real and identical beneath the surface play of signs.[36]

In my view, the current suspicion toward the deep and the hidden is a false dawn. Philosophy cannot survive without some sense of the *je ne sais quoi,* which is built in advance into the Greek word *philosophia*: referring to the love of wisdom, not to wisdom as something directly accessible. Reality is not directly available either to reason or to the senses, which means that the old rationalist/empiricist dispute is beside the point. Nor do we touch the world directly in everyday pragmatic behavior, despite the fashion in present-day philosophy of focusing on "practices."[37] Socrates was neither logician nor natural scientist nor pragmatist, but a professor of ignorance, even if he pursued a "learned ignorance" (Nicholas of Cusa) different from flat-out unknowing.[38] In modern philosophy this healthy version of ignorance was revived by Kant's unknowable thing-in-itself. And while the *Ding an sich* was quickly dismissed by Kant's successors, his aesthetic theory had better luck, probably due to the inherent difficulty of shoehorning artworks into explicit rational formulae. Although attempts have not been lacking, it would be strange to reduce an artwork either to its physical components or to a sum of literal propositions, except perhaps in outlier cases—Marcel Duchamp comes to mind—where the artist purposely toys with such reductions. But even here, if a Duchampian readymade is to act as an artwork rather than as a clever literalist stunt—and I believe it can—it must command the beholder's aesthetic involvement. And this requires more than the mere stipulation that something is an artwork if the artist says it is.[39]

At the very least, the *je ne sais quoi* refers to something withheld from direct human access, and the arts simply cannot exist without such a thing. Let's begin with visual art, given that Sullivan's backdoor effort at a composite purity of form and function is initially harder to judge. The interest in taste and the "I know not what" seems to have originated outside the arts, in the ethical and political spheres.[40] The crafty Spanish Jesuit Baltasar Gracián is surely most famous as the author of *The Art of Worldly Wisdom.* His lesser-known debut book, *The Hero,* published in 1637, contains the following fine words:

> If the sun were to refuse its kindly Warmth to the Earth,
> it would produce no Fruits; and if a Man chances to want

this *Je ne sais quoi*, all his fine Qualities are dead and insipid; so that it is not so much a Circumstance, or any outward Property, as it is in the Being and the Essence of the Thing itself. . . . Thus, for instance, we perceive in a Captain a *Je ne sais quoi* of lively Intrepidity, that inspires his Soldiers with Courage and Assurance. In like manner, we perceive in a Monarch, seated on his Throne, a *Je ne sais quoi* of august Appearance, that strikes us with an awful Respect. . . . In a word, this *Je ne sais quoi*, this certain something, without wanting any thing itself, enters into every thing to give it a Worth and Value. It enters into Politicks, into Learning, into Eloquence, into Poetry, into Trade, and is equally found in the Conditions of both high and low.[41]

Early in the following century, the philosopher Leibniz opposes this notion: "Likewise we sometimes see painters and other artists correctly judge what has been done well or badly; yet they are often unable to give a reason for their judgment but tell the inquirer that the work which displeases them lacks 'something, I know not what.'" The difference is that the rationalist Leibniz views this recourse to the unknown as a sign of ignorance in the bad or non-Socratic sense. Whereas Gracián—like Kant—does not think that the unknown element in things can be transferred directly into knowledge, Leibniz sees a perfect continuum between such "confused" aesthetic judgments and "clear" rational ones. As he puts it: "It is certain that the concepts of these [sensory] qualities are composite and *can be resolved*, for they certainly have their causes."[42] Stated differently, Leibniz is a literalist and Gracián is not. But while Leibniz deserves our esteem for his powerful imagination and speculative gambler's streak, and while his vision of the cosmos is as broad as one could wish, we will see that his confidence in "resolving" aesthetic judgments by showing them to be merely confused versions of fully rational ones is misplaced.

In a later chapter I will explain why literalism is wrong-headed, both in the arts and elsewhere. Literalism, of which rationalism is just one especially prominent subspecies, is effectively the notion that we can adequately describe any given entity by enumerating an appropriate set of qualities: we know a thing completely when we know all the qualities that truly belong to it. The first problem with this doctrine is that objects—of whatever kind—have at best a loose relationship with at least some of their qualities. Husserl's phenomenology is especially insightful as to how the features of an experienced object shift constantly from one moment to the next without the object itself disappearing or changing; this apple remains this very apple even if its palpable qualities alter drastically throughout an hour or more of our observing it in the shifting sunlight. Of course, Husserl also holds that every object has certain *essential* features that it needs in order to go on being what it is, and holds further that these are accessible to the intellect if not to the senses. In short, he resolves the object/quality tension by way of a taxonomical distinction. Unlike Hume—his true enemy—Husserl is not a literalist when it comes to sense experience, given that sensual objects are not reducible to bundles of qualities but are "something more" that endures through all manner of changes in these qualities. Nonetheless, Husserl is very much a literalist when it comes to the ability of the thinking mind to "resolve" an object into its essential qualities by intellectual means. In this respect he is no less a rationalist than Leibniz, despite his far greater interest in the subtlest flickerings of human experience. Stated differently, Husserl creates a taxonomy of two zones of reality: the realm of sensual experience is nonliteral, yet there is a deeper foundational layer—directly accessible to the mind—where objects can be literally known. The reason this half-literalist ambition of phenomenology fails is seen most clearly by Heidegger: reality itself always withdraws, or *withholds itself* from relation.

Nonetheless, the OOO way of clarifying the point is different from Heidegger's own. Imagine that we were able to produce a perfect literal model of a given object. This is what

Merleau-Ponty attempts when he says that "the house itself is not the house seen from nowhere, but the house seen from everywhere."[43] In brief, he maintains that the house is nothing more than all possible views of it added into a sum. I hope the problem with this claim will be obvious. One can live in a house, or one can tear it down. But one cannot live in or tear down any *view* of a house, nor is this any more successful if we add all possible views of it into a giant pile of possibilities. Simply put, the different views of a house are possible *because it is a house,* rather than the house existing because there are many views of it. If we shift our scenario from a house made of views to a chemical element and its properties, something analogous happens. To compile a list of all the properties of an atom of gold is not to create such an atom; more generally, to know all aspects of a thing—assuming this were possible—is not to create that thing. The Oxford philosopher Stephen Mulhall deems this argument absurd and attacks it in the following words: "[Harman's] conviction about the inherent inaccessibility of reality seems ultimately to rest on assuming that genuine knowledge of an object would have to take the form of becoming wholly and fully identical with that object."[44] But this is precisely not what I assume. The claim is not that we cannot know a thing without being it, but that we *can* know a thing without being it—which just goes to show the difference between knowledge and reality. Hence any genuine realism must uphold the *je ne sais quoi,* which is not unknowable *per se,* but only unknowable by literal means.

At any rate, British aesthetic theory by the 1700s was becoming especially aware of the inherent problems with any rationalist or literalist approach. In 1692, the well-traveled former diplomat William Temple wrote as follows in praise of Chinese gardens:

> Among us [Europeans], the beauty of building and planting is placed chiefly in some certain proportions, symmetries, or uniformities; our walks and our trees ranged so as to

Yuyuan Garden, Shanghai. Creative Commons Attribution-Share Alike 3.0 Unported. Photograph by J. Patrick Fischer.

answer one another, and at exact distances. The Chineses [*sic*] scorn this way of planting. . . . Their greatest reach of imagination is employed in contriving figures, where the beauty shall be great, and strike the eye, but without any order or disposition of parts that shall be commonly or easily observed.[45]

British aesthetic writers of the 1750s were still heavily under Chinese influence, as seen in this stirring account from the Swedish-born William Chambers, who visited China three times:

As the Chinese are not fond of walking, we seldom meet with avenues or spacious walks, as in our European plantations:

the whole ground is laid out in a variety of scenes, and you are led, by winding passages cut in the groves, to the different points of view. . . . Sometimes they make a rapid stream, or torrent, pass under the ground, the turbulent noise of which strikes the ear of the new-comer, who is at a loss to know from whence it proceeds: at other times they dispose the rocks, buildings, and other objects that form the composition, in such a manner that the wind passing through the different interstices and cavities, made in them for that purpose, causes strange and uncommon sounds. They introduce into these scenes all kinds of extraordinary trees, plants, and flowers, form artificial and complicated echoes, and let loose different sorts of monstrous birds and animals. In their scenes of horror, they introduce impending rocks, dark caverns, and impetuous cataracts rushing down the mountains from all sides; the trees are ill-formed, and seemingly torn to pieces by the violence of tempests; some . . . [appear] as if they had been brought down by the fury of the waters; others look as if shattered and blasted by the force of lightning; the buildings are some in ruins, others half-consumed by fire. . . . They frequently erect mills, and other hydraulic machines, the motions of which enliven the scene. . . . In compositions of this kind the Chinese surpass all other nations. The making them is a distinct profession; and there are at Canton, and probably in most other cities of China, numbers of artificers constantly employed in this business.[46]

At an earlier moment in the discussion, in 1712, Joseph Addison had distinguished between the "Great," the "Uncommon," and the "Beautiful."[47] It is not surprising that he classifies the effects of Chinese gardens under the heading of the "Uncommon," for as Chambers reports, the Chinese gardens he saw were relatively small. Addison's term "Great" refers to scenes of far greater scale, which will later become "the sublime" in the variant approaches of Kant and Edmund Burke. In fact, an excessive appeal to "greatness" is in my view the biggest problem with Kant's theory of the sublime: "We call *sublime* what is *absolutely large*."[48] With the word "absolutely," the sublime is treated as a kind of infinity that takes us immeasurably far beyond human comprehension. And paradoxically enough, this infinite turns out to be an anthropocentric concept that effectively reduces the formless to the conditions of human experience, since we too easily pride ourselves on being able to conceive of the infinite at all. When Timothy Morton introduces his concept of "hyper-objects," meaning objects massively distributed in space or time relative to the human scale, he offers the following critique of the infinite, and by extension of the sublime: "Infinity is far easier to cope with. Infinity brings to mind our cognitive powers. . . . But hyperobjects are not forever. What they offer instead is *very large finitude.* I can think infinity. But I can't count up to one hundred thousand."[49] This provides grounds for suspicion of Addison's divide between the "Great" and the "Uncommon," reading the former as the sublime and the latter as closer to beauty. For the reasons given by Morton, we should distrust the recent prestige of the sublime and focus instead on the specific strange effects wrought by "winding passages cut in the groves," along with "mills, and other hydraulic machines, the motions of which enliven the scene."

The Power of Zero

We close this chapter with some new terminology of great relevance to this book, though it takes us outside architecture and back into philosophy. One of the most heated disputes in present-day philosophy of mind is that between so-called first-person and third-person approaches to mental life. While countless authors are involved in the dispute, it will suffice to mention just two of them: David Chalmers and Daniel Dennett, who represent two extremes of the discussion. Chalmers speaks of "the hard problem" when discussing the first-person experience of consciousness.[50] It is "hard" in the sense that there is no obvious way to account for one's own direct experience of mental life in terms drawn from the natural sciences. In first-person experience I know what it is like to be me, you know what it is like to be you, and a dog or bird presumably knows immediately what it is like to be itself. By this account, any entity is conscious if there is something "it is like" to be that entity. Chalmers goes so far as to suggest that even a thermostat might be conscious, though in the eyes of many readers he is pushing his luck, and Chalmers himself hesitates to defend a full-blown pan-psychism that would treat even rocks and dust as conscious.[51]

Naturally, hard-core rationalists are horrified by suggestions of this sort. Most of them wish to limit consciousness to a much smaller roster of obviously sentient animals, if they even go that far. But alongside these are others who deny the importance—or even existence—of irreducible first-person experience at all. Dennett is a good example, since for him there is no "hard problem" in the first place. As he sees it, mental life can be exhaustively defined in terms of (a) subpersonal neurological components plus (b) observable outward behavior, and there is nothing more to the question than that.[52] Restated in OOO terminology, Dennett thinks that first-person consciousness can be undermined and overmined out of existence. Third-person scientific description—through a team effort led by neuroscience and behavioral psychology—will someday tell us all there is to know about mental life. Chalmers responds in part by postulating "zombies" who might behave exactly like humans for third-person observers despite having no conscious life at all, a case that Dennett's theory cannot easily handle.[53]

In this particular struggle I side with Chalmers and the "hard problem" contingent, though I hold that they are wrong in limiting it to consciousness.[54] Not just mental life but *everything else as well* is inexplicable through the combination of downward and upward reduction that Dennett recommends. Yet there is still a difficulty for the hard problem approach: namely, first-person experience is no less

relational than the third-person kind. First-person advocates are right to conclude that mental experience is something real, and that nothing is solved by deflecting it into
questions of brain science and public behavior. Even so, conscious life is not simply what I experience of it, since I can
be as wrong about myself as about anything else; the "I" is
not primarily an experience but a surplus that makes such
experience possible. And here the third-person scientistic
approach is right to claim that introspection is just as fallible
as any description of nonhuman entities from the outside. We
easily fail in interpreting our own motivations, and sometimes even our sensory experience. Life simply cannot be
identified with what we experience of it. But if first-person
experience always falls short in interpreting itself, the same
holds for third-person experience: appeals to "science" are
appeals to knowledge, and we have seen that this amounts
to reducing objects—whether downward or upward—to
bundles of qualities. Nor is it enough to claim, in a feigned
spirit of balanced fairness, that both first-person and third-
person experience exist without each being reducible to the
other, as argued in different ways by A. S. Eddington and
Wilfrid Sellars.[55] When Eddington claims that there are "two
tables"—the one of experience and the other of science—
and Sellars contends that we must accept both the "manifest
image" and the "scientific image" of things, they are both
still reducing the world to a set of images that, in principle, can be known directly. Since neither first-person nor
third-person description is enough to account for the mind
or anything else, we need an indirect *zero-person* approach
to tunnel our way toward the surplus in things, which resists
exhaustion by the combined force of both kinds of images.[56]
By analogy we also need a zero-person approach to architecture, one where both form and function recede from their
relation to humans.[57] Note that this does not mean "architecture without humans." We are asking about architecture
without human beholders, not without human ingredients,

though it remains to be seen what zero-architecture might be like.[58]

We should also consider the element of *time*, which is far more pronounced in architecture than in visual art. At least with traditional painting, there is a sense in which the entire work is present to the beholder at once. In fact, this is one of the keys to Fried's critique of minimalism in "Art and Objecthood," and is the very reason he was so appalled in the 1960s by Tony Smith's aestheticized report of driving down the unfinished New Jersey turnpike.[59] For Fried the experience of visual art should be instantaneous; extending it in time reduces it to a kind of theatrical performance. This is precisely why he rejects minimalism, with its ominously lit and positioned shapes. I remember a campus gallery show from my undergraduate years that provided an illuminating display of this principle. In the work in question, only one narrow horizontal line of a painting was visible, though the beholder could turn a dial that moved the line up or down in order to see different portions of the painting in sequence. The effect was both comical and intriguing, and resulted more in a conceptual work than in a painting in the strict sense. With a sculpture the element of time is already somewhat stronger, since one can view it from numerous angles, as Greenberg complains when reviewing the three-dimensional work of Edgar Degas: "His bronzes . . . depend just a little too much on the spectator's finding just the right point of vantage."[60] With literature the temporal element is stronger, and in theater and film—at least in its movie-house days—it becomes so strong that one cannot dip into and out of the work as one pleases; instead, one must commit oneself to experiencing the work at a single, uninterrupted clip of two hours or more. What about architecture? One of Giedion's major theses in *Space, Time and Architecture* is that modernist architecture adds a temporal element foreign to classical building. The young Eisenman makes the same case, but for architecture *tout court*:

> To understand architectural form we must introduce the notion of movement and postulate that an experience of architecture is the sum of a large number of experiences, each one of them apprehended visually (as well as through the other senses), but accumulated over a much longer time span than is required for the initial appreciation of a pictorial work.[61]

As we saw in chapter 1, Eisenman's former student Lynn made even more explicit appeal to time in the 1990s with his discussion of *movement* in architecture.[62] I cite Eisenman here for his earlier and in some respects more basic insight—however atypical of his later views—that all architecture must be experienced in time.[63] This entails, perhaps surprisingly, that architectural time must be actively "zeroed" along with its form and function. After all, what is in question here is not anyone's accidental first-person experience of walking through the various parts of a building over the course of an hour or two, but an ideal sense in which the parts of a building are *essentially* spread out in time no less than in space. Stated differently, time is an inherent aspect of architectural form, and hence must be reconceived in a nonrelational way. For the purposes of this book, to "zero" something means to subtract it from its relations.[64] Zero-form is not hard to grasp once we take a distance from the customary visual sense of form and turn our attention to something more like the substantial forms of Aristotelian philosophy. Zero-function seems harder to fathom, since by "function" I mean any sort of relation, not just the technical kind. To ask about zero-function is to ask about relations subtracted from relationality, and this is a paradox faced only by architecture, since Kant walls off visual art from relation altogether.

Here it is worth recording the insights of Rossi from a section of his great book *The Architecture of the City* titled "Critique of Naïve Functionalism"; for OOO purposes, this phrase might be rewritten as "Critique of Naïve Relationism."[65] For Rossi, deeper than function is form, and deeper than form is type. "No type can be identified with only one form. . . . Type is the very idea of architecture, that which is closest to its essence."[66] Function cannot be primary, since there are "important urban artifacts whose function has changed over time or for which a specific function does not even exist."[67] Moreover, "if urban artifacts were constantly able to reform and renew themselves simply by establishing new functions, the values of the urban structure, as revealed through its architecture, would be continuous and easily available. The permanence of buildings and forms would have no significance."[68] Whereas present-day philosophy habitually assumes that relations are a guaranteed source of dynamic flux, Rossi shows a clearer head on this issue: functionalist classifications "presuppose that all urban artifacts are created to serve particular functions in a static way and that their structure precisely coincides with the function they perform at a certain moment." A relation simply is what it is right now, but an object can serve one role at one time and another later on, which shows that there is no dynamism in the world without a nonrelational surplus somewhere in the picture.

Against any overdetermination of things by their relations, Rossi contends later in the book that "a specific urban artifact persists together with [its form], and that it is precisely a form that persists through a set of transformations which constitutes an urban artifact par excellence."[69] On the same note, "to think of a persistent urban artifact as something tied to a single period of history constitutes one of the greatest fallacies of urban science."[70] And later: "The world of architecture can be seen to unfold and be studied as a logical succession of principles and forms more or less autonomous from the reality of *locus* and history."[71] The autonomy of form becomes especially clear in the case of durable urban monuments, which partly rise above the normal course of history and even the notion of context. In Rossi's fine words: "As for the term *context*, we find that it is mostly an impediment to research. To context is opposed the idea of the monument. Beyond its historically determined existence, the monument has a reality that can be subjected to analysis."[72]All of this is helpful and inspiring, and makes a fine fit with OOO's model of an enduring object that supports countless different relations rather than becoming something different as these relations alter from moment to moment. Nonetheless, Rossi seems to eliminate functions from the picture outright rather than finding some way to zero them—as if he were assuming that function could never be monumentalized. Thus he remains tacitly intimidated by Kant's rejection of function, when the right way to preserve the honor of architecture would be to formalize function while still keeping it distinct from the form. Failing at the first task means conceding Kant's argument that architecture is excluded from the inner sanctum of aesthetics. Failing at the second amounts to "saving" architecture by claiming it is just another form of visual art, entirely uncontaminated by inessential functions.

3 OBJECT-ORIENTATION

HEIDEGGER, DERRIDA, AND DELEUZE ARE THREE VERY DIFFER-
ent philosophers; we have seen that the same is true of their
respective influences on architecture. The most glaring point
that unifies the three is that none of them attempts any
articulation of reality *in profundum*: none has the capacity
or even desire to carve out the details of the deep structure
of the world. The reasons are different in each case. For
Derrida there is no such thing as depth in the first place,
since anything deep would necessarily claim—falsely, in
his eyes—to be "self-present," a self-identical unit impossibly submerged beneath the ubiquitous play of signs. For
Deleuze, by contrast, there is something like a dimension of
depth, even if he would not want to put it that way. Despite
his allegiance to immanence, the Deleuzian virtual is deeper
than the actual; the latter is defined not only as a surface but
as a sterile one without causal power.[1] Though we frequently
hear from Deleuzians that the virtual is both heterogeneous
and continuous, any specific articulation of that hetero-
geneity proves elusive in the face of its primal continuity.

Architecturally speaking, consider the case of Patrik Schumacher, long one of the major figures at Zaha Hadid Architects in London. It is true that Schumacher's case for the design theory he calls parametricism appeals primarily to the social theorist Niklas Luhmann rather than Deleuze. Nonetheless, Schumacher finds himself in what sounds very much like a Deleuzian design impasse: "the insertion of all the necessary apertures (windows and doors) within the research program of Folding/Parametricism—privileging seamlessness and the integration of skin and skeleton within a single structural surface—represents a formidable challenge to the ingenuity of the avant-garde designer."[2] When one is deeply committed to a continuist philosophy in which everything shades slowly into everything else without sudden breaks, it is difficult indeed to account for the definite cutoff points embodied in apertures, thresholds, entries, walls, and corridors—not to mention discrete functions more generally.

Turning at last to Heidegger: his thinking obviously contains the overwhelming depth dimension of *Sein*, or Being, which withdraws into a state of concealment, veiling, sheltering, preserving, and other synonymous terms. Nonetheless, Heidegger has an unfortunate tendency to conflate his guiding distinction between concealed and revealed with a rather different divide between one and many. This remains true even of his most advanced effort to account for individual entities in positive terms, in the brilliant late work "The Thing."[3] After all, this essay's fourfold treatment of things—earth, sky, gods, and mortals—contains the term "earth," which cannot plausibly be read as having any genuine plurality to it. Instead, it is more like a pre-Socratic *apeiron* unifying all things in a single whole, and thus belongs to the same family of ideas as Lynn's Deleuze-inspired notion of the blob. For Heidegger, all entities are ultimately rooted in a same and single earth that prevents them from ever being fully discrete; it is "sky" where individuality can be found. Admittedly, he never explicitly states that there is a primordial whole called Being and that individual entities are broken away from it only due to human thought, as does the pre-Socratic thinker Anaxagoras. But as is so often the case, Heidegger's half-stated tendency in this direction is brought into the open by one of his most talented intellectual heirs: the early Levinas of the prisoner-of-war period.[4] Explicitly for Levinas, as implicitly for Heidegger, reality itself is a rumbling totality broken into parts only by the derivative labors of human thought.

It is certainly not automatic that architects inspired by given philosophers will always exhibit flaws or limitations in their design work analogous to those in their favorite thinkers. For instance, Heidegger speaks rarely and unconvincingly of human sensual experience, but the architectural phenomenology that admires him turns sensuality into a veritable specialty, thanks in large part to the additional influence of Merleau-Ponty. Yet it is doubtless the case that what I have called "articulation in depth" is also missing from the three architectural trends just described. Architectural phenomenology is so devoted to a nearly solipsistic personal experience that anything subsensory tends to be lost, let alone anything social, ethical, or political.[5] Deconstructivism is so focused on what is disruptive and explicitly legible as such, on presenting conceptual paradoxes to the mind, that it cannot really give us a self-enclosed thing, whatever its insistence on doing so. The architectural thing is there before us as a wound to humans, or perhaps merely to "humanism," and harbors no private dimension of its own. Unnerving though these buildings may sometimes be, they contain nothing that humans cannot handle and master. Beyond this, to argue—in a nearly Duchampian manner—that the conceptual is somehow deeper than the sensual is to relapse philosophically into Husserl's position, which misses even Heidegger's demonstration that perception and conception equally reduce the things to their presence for us. Continuism, by contrast—let us give that name to the tradition of Deleuze—can toy with quasi-articulate forms all it likes. But it really just offers spur-of-the-moment solutions to articulation in depth and on the surface, for it always has the alibi at hand of generating *ad hoc* local differences wherever it wants, and claiming that these are merely local intensities along a "heterogeneous yet continuous" gradient. If it were merely a matter of architects following one of these philosophers too closely, this would be nothing more than a trivial career mistake. The bigger problem is found in the architectural consequences of that mistake: Schumacher's admitted uncertainty as to where to locate apertures, Eisenman's active subversion of convenience in the name of theoretical statement, or Zumthor's construction of spas that appeal to the tingling skin and awestruck eyes but tacitly censor whatever lies beyond reach.

The question is whether OOO can do anything better for architecture than inspire overly literal designs of its own: encouraging the production of "mysterious things with variable outlines," as Scharmen put it.[6] Indeed, there is an entire camp in the discipline that wants philosophy—and most other intruders—to leave the room altogether. In the words of Zeynep Çelik Alexander: "The eyes of the design disciplines are no longer on such fields as philosophy, literary criticism, or comparative literature," even if they are now open to neurology and other scientific fields.[7] Fashions will change and winds will shift; bridges are burned and sometimes rebuilt. But no two disciplines are either inherently connected or intrinsically disjunct. Insofar as all branches of human thought must deal in some way with reality, it often happens that two or more disciplines encounter each other on the shores of the same island. Before deciding whether OOO is fruitful in architectural terms, we should first ensure that all readers of this book have some idea of what the object-oriented standpoint is.

Realism in the Wilderness

Although OOO dates to the late 1990s, it became better known to the public following the 2007 "Speculative Realism" workshop in London.[8] The label was meant as an umbrella term to cover four independent efforts to revive philosophical realism within the Continental tradition. Within this tradition, which is shaped primarily by recent French and German authors, realism had long been held in low esteem. Such leading Continental heroes as Husserl and Heidegger had generally treated the existence of a world beyond human awareness as a "pseudoproblem." After all, we are always already outside ourselves in paying attention to objects in the world (Husserl), or involved in a pretheoretical use of tools that become explicit only when they break or otherwise go wrong (Heidegger).[9] It is true that Nicolai Hartmann—a contemporary of Heidegger—had argued for a more robustly realist position, but the fact that Hartmann was so fully eclipsed at the time by his peers is evidence of the low repute of realism in Continental thought; the first signs of a Hartmann renaissance have only begun to appear in recent years.[10] In Italy in the early 1990s, Maurizio Ferraris took a daring realist turn that put him at odds with the relativist Gianni Vattimo, his former professor.[11] In 2002 DeLanda's *Intensive Science and Virtual Philosophy* openly made the case for a realist Deleuze and Guattari; in the same year, my own *Tool-Being* did this for Heidegger. It should also be added that the "realist" turn and the famous "materialist" turn do not entirely overlap. Realism asserts only that something exists independent of us, without necessarily holding that it must be "matter"; for instance, DeLanda defends the centrality of matter, while I deny its existence altogether.[12] By the same token, materialists need not even be realists. Note that the most systematic of the New Materialists, Karen Barad, is committed not to a mind-independent reality but to the joint construction of reality by the universe and the mind, as in the physics of Niels Bohr on which she relies so heavily.[13]

Despite numerous fatal differences among the Speculative Realists—the group would dissolve in just two years' time—a point we had in common was our firm opposition to what Quentin Meillassoux calls "correlationism," a term similar to my own "philosophy of access."[14] According to the correlationist, we cannot think the world without human thought or human thought without the world, but only a primordial correlation of the two. Here already we recognize a portrait of Husserl and Heidegger, with their respective correlations of thought and intentional object, or *Dasein* (human being) and *Sein* (being itself). Not much time was needed for the Speculative Realists to realize that we were in disagreement about the best way to escape the correlate, due to our differing diagnoses of its chief drawback. For Meillassoux, the main problem is that the correlate leaves us stranded in human finitude, closing us off in a circle of fideistic belief, thereby replacing the old pre-Kantian dogmatism with a new kind of fanaticism. Meillassoux was eager to establish a new form of access to the absolute, through an ingenious argument for the absolute necessity of contingency in nature and a fervent commitment to mathematical reason as a way of regaining the primary qualities of things. By contrast, OOO continued to argue that finitude is insurmountable, and that Kant's basic mistake was not to posit a thing-in-itself beyond all human access, but to leave this as a special problem for humans rather than expanding it into a finitude that haunts inanimate object–object relations as well. In this way, Speculative Realism fractured rather quickly into rationalist versions granting priority to mathematics or natural science (Meillassoux and Brassier, respectively) and nonrationalist versions for which thought is just another product of reality rather than an ontologically unique knowledge-bearing position (Iain Hamilton Grant and OOO). So far it is safe to say that the rationalist approach has found somewhat more favor among academic philosophers, while nonrationalist Speculative Realism has dominated interdisciplinary references to this school, including in architecture.

One important contemporary thinker who has influenced OOO alone, with no discernible impact on the other branches of Speculative Realism, is Bruno Latour.[15] Of especial interest here is that Latour and Meillassoux both hold that Kant is the most disastrous influence on modern philosophy, but say so for opposite reasons.[16] For Meillassoux, Kant was the major founder of correlationism in philosophy—even if Hume was the first—and Kant fails precisely through creating an artificial admixture of reality and our access to it.[17] Namely, the great German philosopher holds that we are able to know the world only according to space, time, and the twelve categories of human understanding. This leaves us stranded in the finitude that Meillassoux abhors, and also leads to the famous impossibility of making any statements about the world beyond the sphere of human access to it. German Idealism might seem to have overcome this bind by arguing that any thought of the thing-in-itself is ipso facto a thought, so that the thought/world distinction collapses into a unified space where everything is equally penetrable by dialectical reason; yet it holds firm to the interaction of thought and world as the proper homeland of philosophy. Most commentators have overlooked that Meillassoux *admires* the correlationist argument against the Kantian thing-in-itself.[18] Even so, he aims to provide a new way of discussing reality itself without imploding it into the sphere of thought, in a way that German Idealism never even attempts. Whereas the Kantian thing-in-itself exists beyond all thought, Meillassoux holds it to be perfectly thinkable, but as still "in-itself" in the sense that it can both predate and exceed the life span of the human species. In this way Meillassoux reintroduces a separation between thought and world that, in his view, correlationism had wrongly effaced.

Latour sees exactly the opposite problem with Kantian

modernism. Modernity, as Latour defines it, is the failed attempt to separate or mutually purify the two great modern poles of thought and world.[19] The failure of the modern rift can be seen above all in its inability to account for "hybrid" entities in which nature and culture are inextricably intertwined. Is the ozone hole natural or cultural? Are strawberries, subjected to centuries of breeding and a more recent period of genetic manipulation, natural or cultural? More than difficult, it is impossible to say. In sum, Latour deems Kant guilty of creating an impossible separation between two branches of reality that are actually inseparable, the opposite reading of Meillassoux's own. In fact, though we might interpret Latour simply as claiming that the two poles are "not always" separable, he actually goes further and asserts that they can never be separated: absolutely everything is a hybrid of thought and world. This can be seen in his oft-repeated and controversial view that entities do not predate their discovery. In a sense, there were no microbes before Louis Pasteur, and no tuberculosis in ancient Egypt even if certain mummies show clear traces of that disease.[20]

One could almost imagine a practicing physicist accepting Meillassoux's philosophy, since its allowance for a mathematizable world existing beyond human thought makes a good fit with the assumptions of natural science, despite his unorthodox view that the laws of nature are entirely contingent. It is harder to imagine a physicist agreeing with Latour, since this would require the heretical notion that the unified electromagnetic force was a hybrid coproduced by Maxwell, or that relativistic gravity did not predate Einstein. For this reason Latour will probably always be shunned by mainstream science; already, he is dismissed by the rationalist wing of Speculative Realism on the very same grounds. For Meillassoux and Brassier, thought-world hybrids could only be sociological distractions from full-blown realism, since the whole point is to subtract the "thought" part from the inherent nature of things. Whereas Meillassoux holds that mathematical reasoning can arrive at the things themselves through a form of "intellectual intuition," Brassier insists— much like his enemy OOO—on a permanent gap between knowledge and reality, though he continues to grant science "maximal authority" nonetheless.[21]

It has also been overlooked that the apparently opposite critiques of Kant made by Meillassoux and Latour share a particular assumption. Namely, both accept modernism's *onto-taxonomical* view that there are two and only two great poles of reality, which might be called thought/world, culture/nature, or human/nonhuman. Heidegger and Derrida criticized "onto-theology" as the notion that reality can be made directly present to thought; for Heidegger this means only that we cannot know reality directly, while Derrida denies the existence of any self-identical reality at all. Although their respective criticisms of onto-theology are a good start, both continue to operate within a Kantian horizon in which thought and world—or their rechristened equivalents—are the two basic terms on the table: object-object interactions apart from their presence to humans play vanishingly little role in the works of either thinker.[22] While Heidegger and Derrida may be outstanding critics of onto-theology, they do not address the root of modern philosophy's problem: the onto-taxonomy that takes thought and world to be the two basic terms of dispute.

But let's return to the difference between Meillassoux and Latour. We have seen that they disagree as to whether the mission of philosophy is to separate the two poles of the correlate by rational means (Meillassoux) or to demonstrate that they are inseparable from the start (Latour). Meillassoux's approach was the usual one in early modern philosophy from René Descartes through Kant: for these first modern thinkers there is a gap between thought and what it confronts, and there are different ways of addressing this gap. From Descartes through Berkeley this always involved some sort of recourse to God as the bridge, a current of thought known as "occasionalism"; in Hume and Kant we find a more secular version of early modernism, in which the human mind itself is the bridge between thought and world. Considered in these terms, Meillassoux is essentially a Hume/Kant early modernist, though unlike them he is troubled by the skeptical consequences and seeks a method of accessing the absolute directly. Latour's own approach is a better match for late modern philosophy, beginning with German Idealism and continuing through the present: a period when the supposed gap between thought and world is dismissed as artificial or unnecessary, or as an outright pseudoproblem.

Against both of these stances, OOO rejects the taxonomical basis of modernism outright. The thought/world pair of correlationism must indeed be rejected, but not for the reason that Meillassoux thinks. It is not because thought somehow contaminates reality, so that we must look back to an ancestral age when thought was not there to poison reality with unreality, or ahead to a postextinction era when human perspectives will no longer be on hand to distort the world. Instead, the point is that the thought/world pair is a *compound* no different in kind from the hydrogen/oxygen bond that gives us water as a new entity in its own right. Water is no more—and no less—a unit than compounds involving humans: love and hate, religious beliefs, historical commitments. These are not just dirty mixtures that conceal the independent nature of their elements, but amount to new realities with their own new properties, just as water is not merely a tainted mixture of two pure chemical elements but an autonomous reality of its own. Stated differently, reality is present *above* every correlate and not just beneath it. Not only is there a tree outside my mind that differs from its appearance to me, but my very relation to the tree is also a reality distinct from myself or the tree alone; this relation is also an object impenetrable to anyone's understanding, including my own. For the same reason, water is not just a relation between two elemental ingredients; it is also an emergent entity over and above hydrogen and oxygen, and thus *more* than the sum of its parts. Conversely, we must join Latour in accepting the existence of hybrids, but again not for the reason he thinks. It is not because every point of reality is a hybrid in which humans are somehow entangled, but because every point is a compound made of more basic elements. Sometimes human thought is one of these elements, though far more often it is not. At any rate, in every compound there are also elements under and beneath their joint interaction, and therefore *less* than the events to which they give rise.

Mysterious Things with Variable Outlines

Concerning the dealings between OOO and architecture, we recall that Scharmen made the following parodic critique: "Graham Harman likes inexhaustible objects, so let's make mysterious things with variable outlines."[23] The problem with this formula is that we can make anything look ridiculous merely by literalizing it in this way. Elsewhere I have shown that the same exercise can be turned against as great a work of literature as *Moby-Dick*: "The hero of the book is a bipolar one-legged skipper who cruises the world from Nantucket with a team of multi-ethnic harpooners."[24] Chuckle along with me, but you will probably still agree that Melville's novel is a classic for the ages. The fact that something can be subjected to literalist vandalism does not render it incapable of anything more than literalism. Furthermore, Scharmen's trick can be played on architects even when no philosopher is anywhere near the scene. Try this on for size: "Le Corbusier liked flexible living spaces, so let's make extensive use of the free plan." Or this: "Palladio liked symmetry and ancient civilization, so let's put evenly spaced Greek or Roman columns on all of our buildings." What makes Scharmen's tweets work so well as comedy is the following general formula: "Famous philosopher X liked Y, so let's design in manner Z expressed as a simpleminded adoption of the theories of X." In other words, Scharmen is simply arguing that it is a bad thing to copy someone else's ideas in vulgar or robotic fashion.

A further issue is that Scharmen's joke tacitly misreads OOO as being solely about hiddenness, though this only gets at a quarter of it. What OOO is really about is *the tension between objects and their qualities,* which takes on four different forms: real objects–sensual qualities (vertical tension), real objects–real qualities (causal tension), sensual objects–sensual qualities (horizontal tension), and sensual objects–real qualities (eidetic tension). What Scharmen calls "mysterious things with variable outlines" fits under what I have just termed the vertical tension, which is just one of the four. Sometimes we sense the qualities of an object, though the object itself remains somewhat inscrutable. This is a fairly basic human experience, one that lies at the heart of aesthetics, and hence it would be strange for architecture to prohibit all use of it simply because a philosopher happens to argue for it. It is certainly true that architects already knew this without my help, since it was cultivated extensively by disciplinary notions of the sublime and the picturesque. Not everything under this heading is new, or needs to be new: Le Corbusier and Mies were raising their buildings on plinths long before Tom Wiscombe argued for the same technique in a OOO setting.[25] Even so, the technique gains in significance when seen as part of a fourfold diagram of object–quality tensions.

The second, horizontal tension unfolds between the sensual object and its sensual qualities. The sensual object is any object I might be experiencing, regardless of whether or not it has a real correlate in the outside world. Bohr's model of the atom is a sensual object, but so too is the most abject hallucination. Such objects also have a patina of shifting qualities accessible not only to our senses but to our intellect and practical handling as well. Pictorial cubism operates within this very tension: Picasso and Braque hide nothing behind the surface plane and simply crowd it with numerous profiles that are initially difficult to integrate. Husserlian phenomenology is also located here, since Husserl denies the existence of things-in-themselves withdrawn from human access and focuses on the tension between objects given in experience and their numerous shifting qualities. Corb's recommended play of volumes under sunlight fits here as well, as does Utzon's drama of semispherical and asymmetrically arranged shells, and—in the more recent OOO idiom—Mark Foster Gage's projected neomedieval skyscraper for the West Side of Manhattan and its detailed carvings, as well as his proposed Desert Resort for the Middle East.[26] Because of this doubly sensual horizontal tension, no withdrawal is even needed for OOO aesthetics to be relevant in a given situation. There may be good aesthetic reasons in a particular case to truncate the dimension of withdrawal: the surface play of the Sydney Opera House would be severely weakened if the shells were rendered more ominous; a picturesque Corb would no longer be Corb, and we would only ruin the gardens at Versailles by adding "impending rocks, dark caverns, and impetuous cataracts."[27] To exploit the horizontal tension for aesthetic purposes, one might make use of changing qualities of light and shadow on the same object at different times, the ambiguous legibility of a given palpable object, targeted overornamentation at specific points, or an emphatic transparency that rules any hidden dimension out of court. Designers themselves must draw on historical knowledge and their own powers of invention to develop the needed techniques. OOO cannot do it for them, but what it can do is show how the horizontal tension fits with its three aesthetic cousins.

The third, eidetic tension is somewhat trickier, since it refers to the tension between a graspable sensual object and its hidden real qualities. Husserl discovered this tension

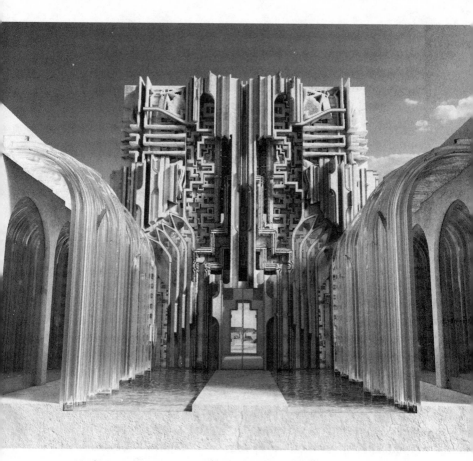

Mark Foster Gage, Desert Resort, Middle East. Copyright Mark Foster Gage Architects / MFGA llc. All rights reserved.

when he noticed that even if we successively strip away the many shifting sensual properties of an apple, there are certain ultimate features that cannot be removed without the apple no longer being what it is. These are its real qualities as opposed to its accidental ones. It will again be left to designers to find ways of capitalizing on the effects of this tension. This will happen only when the architectural object itself is perfectly intelligible and without inherent mystery, while its properties—structural, functional, or otherwise—are left partly shrouded in darkness. If in the vertical tension the aesthetic beholder steps in for the missing object and performs its abandoned qualities, in the eidetic tension the object is right there with us, but our imagination is compelled to ascribe various real qualities to it. A possible example from architecture is OMA's 1991 Villa d'Alva, in which a field of column-like entities holds up a room without it being clear which ones perform genuine structural labor.[28]

The causal tension is the only one of the four that cannot make any direct entry into aesthetics, since it is the tension between real objects and real qualities, neither of them directly accessible. Any attempt to invoke it will verge on the inarticulate, as in the following passage from H. P. Lovecraft's "The Haunter of the Dark": "Ultimate Chaos, at whose centre sprawls the blind idiot god Azathoth, Lord of All Things, encircled by his flopping horde of mindless and amorphous dancers, and lulled by the thin monotonous piping of a daemoniac flute held in nameless paws."[29] While this particular passage borders on a mere list of proper names without clear referent, other approaches may be possible. But one thing we know is that no direct aesthetic expression of the causal tension can be given—in literature, design, or elsewhere. We get at it from a second remove, by way of aesthetic "bank shots." If our goal were to produce such a tension rather than merely understand the example given from Lovecraft, an object's qualities or relations would have to be rendered inscrutable, and some way would need to be found of emphasizing the impenetrability of the object itself to our cognitive efforts. Simon Weir in Australia has made one such effort in his object-oriented meditation on the Corinthian capital.[30] In any case, the phrase "mysterious things with variable outlines" is nowhere close to exhausting what OOO is about. At the very least, one must also add "unmysterious things with mysterious qualities" (eidetic tension),

Corinthian capital, Washington State Capitol Building, Olympia.
Creative Commons Attribution-Share Alike 4.0 International. Photograph by Joe Mabel.

"unmysterious things in a mysterious relation with their unmysterious qualities" (horizontal tension), and "mysterious things with mysterious qualities" (causal tension).

Form Repels Content

Earlier, literalism was defined as the process of mistaking an object for a bundle of qualities. What this definition still misses is not only the "withdrawn" reality of objects but also the loose relation between the object itself and its own features. Another way of putting it is that literalism overemphasizes the content of any given situation. Marshall and Eric McLuhan have probably given the most piercing critique of the limitations of content: linking it with the excessively valued "dialectic" part of the classical trivium, they turn our attention instead to the "rhetoric" part, by which they mean the tacit and unnoticed background environment within which we operate.[31] Elsewhere I have argued that the McLuhans, Heidegger, and Greenberg push the deep medium so far from accessibility that a reversal occurs, and the surface becomes the sole place where anything can actually happen.[32] Yet this does not change the fact that content in isolation cannot be the sole focus of human thought. When it is, we have literalism.

In the realm of comedy, slapstick is the form that most cultured people profess to despise, perhaps because it inhabits a purely physical realm rather than a conceptual one. Yet this disdain for the material realm is both affected and crude. It can be perfectly satisfying to watch Punch swat his companions with a wooden paddle, and when it comes to the Marx Brothers, the mute prankster Harpo is aging much better than the verbal but corny Groucho. What really makes any form of humor low is not its physicality—this is no more than Platonic moralizing—but its literalism. And this is why the pun is truly the lowest form of wit. Counterexamples may exist, but they are merely the exceptions that reveal most clearly the inbuilt handicap that puns must struggle to overcome. Edgar Allan Poe said it best, condemning a deceased author in the following terms: "During the larger portion of his life, he seemed to breathe only for the purpose of perpetrating puns—things of so despicable a platitude that the man who is capable of habitually committing them, is seldom found capable of anything else."[33] What do you call an owl that does magic tricks? Hoo-dini. Get it? Although perfectly wholesome for seven-year-olds, this riddle and its answer are beneath contempt by the standards of adult conversation. The purely accidental overlap between the first syllable of

Harry Houdini's last name and the English onomatopoeia for the call of an owl is so trivial and external as to be repellent to anyone committed to the life of the mind.

Another low form of wit is the easy reversal. When a Paris revolutionary of 1968 transposes the graffiti "God is dead— Nietzsche" into "Nietzsche is dead—God," Slavoj Žižek is right to call this a "reactionary" move.[34] As he puts it, the sheer symmetry of the joke makes it too literal and hence too easy, as if a low-grade comic were merely flipping a face upside down, or "comically" placing a cart before a horse. We can also agree with him that Alenka Zupančič's version of the joke is much better: "God is dead. And, as a matter of fact, I don't feel too well either." Žižek explains this effect as follows: "Crucial for the proper comic effect is not a difference where we expect sameness but, rather, a sameness where we expect difference."[35] This brings us to yet another low form of literalist humor: the excessive use of catchphrases and punch lines by impressionists, which fails for the simple reason that few humans are truly bound to any specific grouping of words. Consider the usual embarrassing imitation of Robert De Niro that begins with his *Taxi Driver* soliloquy: "You talkin' to me? You talkin' to me?" Against this, any genuine comic needs to catch De Niro in his less self-aware moments. The same goes for any Sylvester Stallone that makes cheap recourse to a plaintive "Adrian!" not to mention the nails-on-blackboard cliché of a Schwarzenegger promising, "I'll be back." Rather than turning to canned one-liners of this sort, the skilled impressionist picks up on subtler mannerisms, mining the deep cuts of personal vowel oddities or nervous tics, since these are the traits to which each of us is actually bound over without always knowing it. This tells us something about why architects so often fail when trying to make their buildings closely resemble the shapes of familiar natural or artificial entities, and why other architects are dismayed when the general public likens their buildings to trousers (OMA) or icebergs (Snøhetta).

Good translation of any sort—comical or otherwise—requires not that we attempt the transfer of content from one place to another, but that we try to get the background or "bass line" of an object right. Consider the case of the philosopher Friedrich Nietzsche. A respected reference work summarizes his philosophy, accurately enough, as follows: "He is famous for uncompromising criticisms of traditional European morality and religion, as well as of conventional philosophical ideas and social and political pieties associated with modernity."[36] This is neither false nor even especially banal. And yet, how little it sounds like Nietzsche! Ironically, it would sound much more like him if it were to express the opposite content in a fully Nietzschean style: praising traditional morality and religion and breathing new life into the most mainstream traditional ideas. This would amount to a translation within philosophy itself, retaining Nietzsche's glorious rhetorical sparkle even while reconfiguring this aristocratic atheist into an eloquent defender of the pious Christian everyman. But now, let's shift this experiment to the field of architecture. Imagine that in the year 2050, a delayed Nietzschean tsunami washes over the discipline. Norberg-Schulz's Heidegger and Lynn's Deleuze are now dismissed as unfashionable antiques, and the with-it designer is suddenly immersed in Nietzsche's collected works. Here as with other such movements, we would expect a full range of adaptation, from vapid to ingenious. As the worst imaginable work in this tradition, consider the hypothetical 2053 Nietzsche-Kopf in Weimar: a giant mustachioed head next to the house of the philosopher's death, glaring down the hill menacingly at the former Bauhaus. This would not only be horrible kitsch but might even be politically dangerous, providing a possible gathering point for skinhead militants. Scarcely better is the 2060 Nietzsche monument in Naumburg, made of ten-meter-high letters spelling out "Was mich nicht umbringt, macht mich stärker" (What doesn't kill me makes me stronger).[37] Such a clumsy literal translation of written words into physical form would, of course, be a laughingstock among serious architects. The same for the controversial 2062 Morgenröteturm in central Berlin, replacing the freshly demolished DDR television tower with a "heroic" Renaissance villa, surmounted by an ivory-colored Romanized minaret intermittently and offensively blaring music from Georges Bizet's *Carmen*, so beloved by Nietzsche himself. Although the final project is still horrible, we can detect some progress in this series of buildings. The Nietzsche Head in Weimar is just a point-blank literal imitation of Nietzsche as a physical entity. The Naumburg monument at least extracts a memorable thought from that physical being. And the tower in Berlin is a slight improvement, shying away from straightforward physical or verbal mimicry in favor of a certain Nietzschean esprit. In the critical words of Bryan Norwood: "There must be more steps in the move from ontology's evaluation of the nature of existence to a normative guide for design."[38] Indeed. But how many steps, exactly? No more or fewer than the case requires.

Whenever one thing influences another, there is the danger of what OOO calls undermining, in which the thing itself does not hold, but dissolves in favor of its constituent elements. Consider Bloom's observation from early in *The Western Canon*: "What intimately allies . . . [Ernest] Hemingway, [F. Scott] Fitzgerald, and [William] Faulkner . . . is that all of them emerge from Joseph Conrad's influence but temper it cunningly by mingling Conrad with an American precursor— Mark Twain for Hemingway, Henry James for Fitzgerald, Herman Melville for Faulkner." He draws the conclusion that "strong writers have the wit to transform [their] forerunners into composite and therefore partly imaginary beings."[39] Such combinations help prevent Hemingway, Fitzgerald, and Faulkner from producing mere Conrad pastiche, and thereby assist them in finding their individual voices. Of course there is no guarantee that this will succeed, which is exactly why Bloom specifies that only strong, canonical writers can pull it off. For every Faulkner who combines Conrad and Melville successfully, there might be twenty literary failures inspired by exactly the same pair. A debacle might result, for instance, from trying too literal a union of Conradian surface mannerisms with Melvillian character quirks, so that there is never any "general outline of the whole" (Lovecraft) over and above the various gathered qualities.[40] Either something new and memorable and strong emerges from the whirlpool of influences or it does not. As Kipnis puts it in an architectural context, it depends "not on the success of the project in embodying responses to [its] influences, but on the other contingent effects it continuously generates."[41] DeLanda offers the added criterion that something truly new often has retroactive effects on its own parts.[42] The phenomenon is well known in the literary canon: after Faulkner, we read both Conrad and Melville differently. The same holds often

Andrea Palladio, Villa Rotonda, Vicenza, Italy. Creative Commons Attribution-Share Alike 3.0 Unported. Photograph by Hans A. Rosbach.

enough for architecture. Le Corbusier's landmark Villa Stein at Garches retroactively changes our sense of Palladio's Villa Rotonda, as Colin Rowe explains in his most famous article.[43]

Yet these are tests applied after the fact, when a completed work is measured against the tradition from which it emerges. More useful would be practical rules of thumb for preventing overly literal transport from a philosopher to an architect. This danger exists even for translations within architecture. For every complaint that historical postmodernism fails to digest its precedents, those in the postmodern camp can answer that their opponents offer little more than late modernist pastiche. But our primary concern is with the specific translation between philosophy and architecture. And here I find that Lynn's work does make me read Deleuze differently, while Eisenman also manages to transform my understanding of Derrida: the surest proof that they are not just literal importers of philosophical texts. Architectural phenomenology is less successful in changing my reading of Heidegger, though this may just be because my interpretation of his work has long been fully formed.

As for the opposite direction of transitions from philosophy to architecture, the 1990 exchange of open letters between Derrida and Eisenman sheds some light on this problem. Derrida makes the familiar charge that Eisenman reads him too literally: "This reference to absence is one of the things . . . that has most troubled me in your discourse in architecture. . . . This discourse regarding absence or the 'presence of absence' puzzles me . . . because it deploys so many ruses, complications, and traps."[44] Derrida is also dismayed by how Eisenman appropriates his interpretation of the term *chora* in the Platonic dialogue *Timaeus*: "I am not certain that you have de-theologized and de-ontologized the notion of *chora* as radically as I would have expected. . . . *Chora* is neither the void, as you sometimes suggest, nor absence, nor invisibility."[45] Stripping away his usual fuss and feathers, Derrida's complaint is roughly as follows. In his architecture, Eisenman tries to make absence present, and also—along with Libeskind—tries too hard to create actual voids in his work. Supposedly, both of these gestures are overly literal misreadings of points treated more subtly in Derrida's own philosophy. And yet, I am inclined to take Eisenman's side in this particular debate. For it is less a question of an overly literal reading of Derrida than of a serious effort to translate his work into architectural terms. In a deceptively trenchant critique of Derrida's intellectual project, Eisenman notes that he—unlike Derrida—cannot avoid delivering the goods. The architect too can raise radical questions about the interplay of signs, signifiers, and presence, but "without, at the same time, causing the room to be dark or the building to fall down. This is not the case in language, where you and I can play with *glas* and *post, gaze,* and *glaze* precisely because of the traditional dialectic of presence and absence." He concludes with cutting understatement: "It is improbable to effect in architecture what you do in language."[46]

In fact, there are many possible ways to borrow an influence while canceling the literal status of the borrowing. One is so commonsensical that it usually happens unconsciously, and hardly demands explicit formulation: limiting the scope of one's loan. Picasso's 1937 *Guernica* famously depicts the horrors of the Luftwaffe bombing of that Spanish market town in the same year. Yet it remains silent about other tragic events of 1937, such as the catastrophic flooding of the Ohio River and the infamous *Hindenburg* airship disaster. Borrowing an influence can also be done more consciously, as when architects or others strip down an original model in a "dehumidification" of content that draws our attention to subtler resonances between original and descendant; the architect Michael Young has written effectively on this type of abstraction.[47] In some cases, the content of the original model might be deliberately inverted, ensuring that literalism is suppressed and the style is allowed to shine through;

we have already seen the possible example of a Christian or socialist Nietzsche. But more pertinent to our topic is that an architect might deliteralize Derridean influence by rerouting it through Russian Constructivism, thereby gaining an extra bounce from the gravitational field of that movement—which is precisely what happens in Wigley's 1988 catalog essay. In other instances, the old content might be preserved in enfeebled form, like a weakened virus in a vaccine, as in Claude Debussy's playful mockery of *Tristan und Isolde* in "Golliwog's Cakewalk." One might even use more peripheral features of a model to counteract the model's overly literal influence. Imagine that Deleuzian architects avoided folding and continuity but capitalized instead on his witty call for a "*philosophically* bearded Hegel, a *philosophically* clean-shaven Marx, in the same way as a moustached Mona Lisa," perhaps by deploying an *architecturally* modern Alberti or an *architecturally* historicist Mies.[48] There are many possible strategies for deliteralizing an influence, all of them involving different modes of interference with the original content. Given this abundance of methods, it seems needlessly anxious to exclude philosophers from architectural discourse out of fear that their influence might prove too literal.

4 THE AESTHETIC CENTRALITY OF ARCHITECTURE

IN PREVIOUS CHAPTERS I OCCASIONALLY INVOKED THE SPECIF-ically OOO conception of "formalism." The time has now come to treat of this notion in detail; the reader is warned in advance that this will be a difficult chapter requiring close attention. The most important audience question I ever received at a conference was posed by the organizer of the event. His name was Tom Trevatt, the date was September 9, 2012, and the location was Île de Vassivière, France, located at the exact geographic center of that country. My lecture was titled "Art and Paradox," and though I no longer recall the details of that talk, I will never forget what Trevatt asked in public afterward: "What would an art without humans look like?"[1] Though I was stumped by this query at the time, and for months afterward, the reason behind it was clear enough. Given that I am one of the original group of Speculative Real-ist philosophers, and given that this movement is known for downplaying the modern obsession with human access to the world in favor of a meditation on the world itself, does it not follow that Speculative Realism should advocate an art without the human beholder? After all, this would make a direct analogy with Meillassoux's appeal to an "ancestral" realm of nature predating the existence of all consciousness.[2] It was a long while before I grasped the importance of Trevatt's way of putting the question, and years before I realized that it was a misunderstanding of what OOO—if not the other variants of Speculative Realism—is all about. The present chapter will explain why. After passing through Immanuel Kant's *Critique of Judgment* to the twentieth-century formalist art criticism that owes so much to that classic work, we will emerge on the other side with an awareness of the crucial role of architecture in the aesthetics to come.

Art and Beholder

We saw earlier that Meillassoux and Latour reject the Kantian legacy for opposite reasons. Meillassoux thinks we approach reality itself by subtracting human thought from any situation, while Latour thinks we do so by showing that the human is a component of every reality, thereby changing all "matters of fact" into what he calls "matters of concern."[3] Into which of these two baskets should we place Trevatt's question? Obviously, it belongs in the Meillassoux basket. If Speculative Realism has something to offer the art world, Trevatt seemed to reason, then surely it must be found in somehow *separating* the artwork from humans. The alternative would be a Latourian one, in which the artwork would be inseparable from all the various human and nonhuman negotiations that gave rise to it. Even though Latour has not made this point explicit in the case of visual art, he and Yaneva have stated it plainly enough in their coauthored article on architecture: a building is not a free-standing object disconnected from its creators and users, but a "project" that arose from a specific past and is destined to engage with various unforeseeable human and nonhuman actors in the future.[4]

Trevatt was not the first to propose a Speculative Realist art without humans. Early in the history of the movement, I was delighted when the Polish American artist Joanna Malinowska held a show in 2009–10 titled *Time of Guerrilla Metaphysics,* a reference to the title of my second book.[5] The show was well received, and of course I was happy: already we were having an impact on the art world! I was also delighted with the specific example of human-free art that Malinowska reported to David Coggins in their conversation in *artnet*: "I had a boombox powered by a solar battery playing the recording of [Glenn Gould's] famous [version of Bach's] Goldberg Variations. I installed it in the middle of absolute Arctic nowhere, and it will keep playing until it gets destroyed."[6] This seems to answer Trevatt's question as to what art without humans would look like: simply put an artwork in some location where no human is likely to observe it. But an objection arises. For despite the physical removal of this work from any probable human beholder, the work still fits within the parameters of known forms of conceptual art. After all, Malinowska was still telling a magazine about her piece, thereby placing her work squarely within the thoroughly monitored art world. And even if she had gone another step further, performing that work *without* reporting it to anyone, producing it solely as a private construction in her mind, it would still be there in her memory as an artwork. Note that this would be the case even if she had gone "full Meillassoux," and rather than actually hauling a piece to the middle of Arctic nowhere, had merely stipulated that some long-exploded star from billions of years ago was her artwork. She might even have purposely created an object solid enough to outlast the human species, perhaps by secretly launching a probe deep into outer space, however precarious the funding avenues for such a project might be. Yet both of these options would still be conceptual works for Malinowska, as for anyone else who somehow became aware of them. More generally, to place an artwork at a distance in physical space or time from humans is not enough to create the desired separation. The point of aesthetic realism is different: namely, even when humans are standing there looking directly at an artwork, there is something in it that resists our grasp. And this is precisely the dispute between me and Meillassoux over what the thing-in-itself ought to mean. For the French philosopher, the thing-in-itself becomes in-itself simply by our realizing that it can precede or outlast humans in time; for me, as for Kant, the thing-in-itself exists here and now, through our inability to gain direct access to it whether through mathematics or other means. This is why Meillassoux thinks the problem with Kant is his commitment to human *finitude,* while for me it is his limitation to merely *human* finitude, and his resulting failure to consider that objects are finite for each other as well. Most misunderstandings of Speculative Realism hinge on confusion over this basic disagreement.

This notion of an artwork separate from humans is already active in the aesthetic theories of Kant and his living admirer, the art critic and historian Michael Fried. I have addressed this point elsewhere in two recent works, *Dante's Broken Hammer* (2016) and *Art and Objects* (2020), in which I systematically aired the basic positions of OOO aesthetics for the first time. At the center of those books was not Latour's hybrid but the compound—that is, any entity composed of different ingredients regardless of whether a human is one of them. The goal was to preserve Latour's powerful critique of Kantian onto-taxonomy while avoiding what I take to be Latour's incorrect solution, which simply fuses the two sides of the modern thought/world rift without questioning their basic primacy. This holds even for Latour's recent monumental project on the modes of existence, which remains centered in a suspiciously modern-sounding distinction between "quasi-objects" and "quasi-subjects."[7] In *Dante's Broken Hammer* I argued that Dante the poet was an anticipatory critic of modernism, since his cosmos consists not of humans standing over against a world, but of amorous agents fused with good and bad objects, either loyal or traitorous to them as the case may be. While it might seem that phenomenology is already full of such fusions, Dante grasps the point more clearly than this later movement, thanks to his medieval realist awareness that love is simply one more entity in the cosmos rather than a uniquely special hybrid that fuses two privileged poles. Dante is in fact the perfect anti-Kant: for whereas the latter places reality at such an ungraspable distance that little can be said of it, and advises the human being to take a cautious distance toward both artworks and ethical actions, Dante both advocates and judges our passionate attachments to the various things of the world.

Now, "formalism" is one of those terms—much like "realism" itself—that means different things in different mouths, even if we limit ourselves to the visual arts. I use "formalism" in the Kantian sense of the term, found primarily in his ethical writings, in which a particular portion of reality is taken to be cut off from the rest. His famous *terme d'art* for such splitting is "autonomy," which arises in his ethical writings but lies at the heart of everything he ever penned. What ethical formalism means for Kant is that an act is not strictly ethical unless performed solely from rational duty, rather than from hopes and fears concerning the afterlife, the wish to gain a public reputation for benevolence, or some other motivation. Though I do not recall his using the term "autonomy" in connection with art, his concern that something be considered beautiful in its own right—rather than because of the agreeable sensations it provides, or the conceptual meaning extracted from it—qualifies him as the godfather of aesthetic formalism as well. This is precisely how he is viewed by such formalist critics as Greenberg and Fried, who express a sincere though unjustified wish not to be called formalists.[8] We might also say that Kant's *Critique of Pure Reason* is a formalist work in the ontological sense, given the way it cuts off the noumena from the phenomena, as well as the reverse. OOO seems to be a formalist philosophy in this sense as well, given our interest in the autonomous existence of objects apart from their relations, under penalty of the world becoming a holistic blend in which everything is everything else. Relations between entities are difficult and do not always occur, despite the assumption of relational ontologies—like those of Barad, Latour, and Whitehead—that they are relatively easy and in principle ubiquitous. Hence it might seem strange to appeal to Dante, whose cosmos appears to be a purely relational affair in which humans are damned or saved according to their stance toward the various objects of their love and hate. What this objection misses is that Kant and his formalist heirs wrongly limit formalism to specific cases in which *humans* and *world* are cut off from each other, and this is the onto-taxonomical side of Kant that we must reject. For Dante, by contrast, the loves of each creature are new compound objects distinct from those who observe or judge them. In one sense love is obviously "subjective," but in another, it is a new fact in the world with which lovers themselves and outside observers must come to grips.

An example may be helpful. It would be wrong to deny the autonomous existence of water simply because it is built from a relation between hydrogen and oxygen. There are two reasons for this: (1) The fact that water involves a relation between two elements does not mean that it also relates to everything else. No understanding or use of water, or even blind causal interaction with it, will ever fathom its reality; water is something more than its effects on anything else in the world. And furthermore: (2) Water cannot even be explained away by its internal relation between hydrogen and oxygen, since it exceeds these components in a number of ways, with the most obvious being that it extinguishes fire even though its ingredients can both fuel fire. Stated differently, from the fact that every entity must be a compound— I will not argue the point here—it does not follow that everything is merely a set of relations with other things. No compound object can be fully undermined into its pieces or overmined into its outer effects.[9] The object is a third term that resists both of these forms of knowledge, which happen to be the only two kinds of knowledge there are.[10] This is why cognitive methods other than knowledge are needed to approach the object more adeptly, a number of them already familiar from the arts, not to mention Socratic *philosophia.*

For OOO, everything that exists is a compound without necessarily being a hybrid in Latour's sense, since hybrids require a human ingredient. Any human relation to objects is by definition a hybrid, and this includes all art and architectural works, all political action, and all social facts. Latour famously pushes the matter by treating all facts about nature as hybrids too, since for him any scientific "matter of fact" is really a "matter of concern." Given that complex social processes are needed to discover any fact, Latour holds that they inevitably remain a part of that fact, just as he and Yaneva claim about buildings. This is not the position of OOO, which contends that it is possible to refer to general relativity without referring to the entire history of its discovery, even though I agree with Karl Popper, Imre Lakatos, and the literary critic Bloom that theories and artworks must be understood in dialogue with those they replace, rather than as isolated forms of direct contact with the world.[11] Stated differently, OOO, unlike Latour, is deeply committed to realism in the strong sense of the term, though not in the falsely strong sense that equates realism with the ability to know the world directly. An example of the latter occurs when the analytic philosopher Michael Devitt asserts that realism without *knowledge* of the real is merely a "Fig-Leaf realism," and that bona fide realism requires that the reality outside the mind "(approximately) obey the laws of science."[12] Note that Devitt's view entails the taxonomical assumption that reality means a reality specifically *outside the mind* rather than outside anything else, and the further assumption that what deals with matters outside the mind is natural science rather than art, social science, or the humanities. By contrast, the real for OOO is (1) outside any relation and not just outside human thought, (2) not the exclusive domain of the scientific disciplines, and (3) so real that it can never be identical with any representation of it.

There is a further issue that might prevent the reader from grasping our sense of "compound" unless we confront it at the start. DeLanda begins his influential book *A New Philosophy of Society* by announcing that he will propose a realist theory of society. He notes that realism entails, at the very least, "a commitment to the mind-independent existence of reality." Nonetheless, he is also at pains to add that "in the case of social ontology . . . this definition must be qualified because most social entities, from small communities to large nation-states, would disappear altogether if human minds ceased to exist."[13] Is there a contradiction, then, in wanting to give a theory of mind-independent reality about social reality, which is itself mind-dependent? Of course not, since the supposed contradiction mixes two different senses of "mind-independence." When the human mind is a necessary component of some reality, let's refer to it as an *ingredient* of that reality. Just as DeLanda says, the mind is always an ingredient of society, and the same is true of art and architecture. But in cases where something exists quite apart from whether a mind is observing it, let's borrow Fried's term and refer to the mind as a *beholder* rather than an ingredient of that reality. DeLanda marks the same difference on his opening page, when he says that by a realist theory he means only that society "must assert the autonomy of social entities from the conceptions we have of them." In short, "mind-independent" can mean either *human-ingredient-independent* or *human-beholder-independent,* and realism only entails a commitment to the latter. This needs to be mentioned since—in the rationalist wing of Speculative Realism—there are those who assert we must focus on natural science *as opposed* to the humanities, social sciences, and the arts, as if to discuss objects containing human ingredients automatically leads to antirealism. But hybrid entities are no less real than natural ones: the reality of the Roman Empire is not inferior to that of a boron atom, even if the former is more fleeting and less susceptible to mathematization.

To avoid further misunderstanding, we should also distinguish between the OOO sense of formalism and different uses of the term by influential theorists of my own generation and later. My favorite of these is found in Caroline Levine's book *Forms,* which attempts to revive the long-despised term "formalism" among literary critics. What is powerful in Levine's book is her argument that literary formalism need not commit itself, as in the past, to purely textual questions at the expense of sociopolitical ones. For it is not just texts but human life as a whole that displays countless organizing forms; this is true of school disciplinary routines and national constitutions no less than of stanzas in a poem. Where I differ from Levine is that she tends to interpret such forms in relational terms, along the lines of Latourian actors or James J. Gibson's "affordances," whereas OOO is also interested in forms quite apart from how they interact with other forms.[14] Also of interest is both Tom Eyers's and Paul Livingston's use of the term "formalism" to pertain to "impasses of formalization," as in the self-reflexive failures demonstrated by Kurt Gödel's famous proof, Derrida's deconstruction, Jacques Lacan's psychoanalytic model of the Real as a trauma to the symbolic order, Alain Badiou's theory of events, and Žižek's conception of parallax.[15] The problem is that all such impasses, and Eyers's and Livingston's treatment of them, rely too heavily on the onto-taxonomical conception of the human subject as somehow ontologically unique. As a rule, there is no "realism" or "formalism" in the OOO sense unless a theory applies equally well to object-object interactions in the absence of any subject; where such

cosmological scope is lacking, one remains within the confines of modern philosophy while leaving its basic taxonomy
intact. More generally, whenever "self-reflexivity" is taken
to be a privileged instance for thought, there is a confusion
between mind as ingredient and mind as beholder: two distinct realities that do not coincide just because we happen to
look in a mirror.

The Cellular Structure of Art

The three branches of Kantian formalism arise from his
three great books, published from 1781 to 1790, each of which
found a later critic equal to the occasion. The *Critique of Pure
Reason* gives us Kant's general ontology, the *Critique of Practical Reason* his ethics, and the *Critique of Judgment* his aesthetic
theory (along with some crucial reflections on biology).
I have already mentioned that Latour provides the most serious challenge to the First Critique, with his introduction of
hybrids. Max Scheler is the one who confronted Kant's ethics
with a probing critique of ethical formalism. More recently,
Fried was compelled to depart from Kantian aesthetics in
spite of his own deeply Kantian instincts; Fried was never
a Hegelian, despite Robert Pippin's attempt to contrast him
with Greenberg in this way.[16]
     The lesson to be drawn from the respective challenges to
Kant by Latour, Scheler, and Fried is that the basic unit of
philosophy must be reconsidered along Dantean lines.[17] The
modern topography, which we are now obliged to oppose,
looks something like this: there is a subject on top of reality and an object on the bottom. This remains the case no
matter what shape is given to the latter. In one sort of philosophy, that object is taken to be something lying *deeper*
than our explicit perceptions or relations: whether it be
Kant's unknowable thing-in-itself, Meillassoux's mathe-
matically accessible thing-in-itself, Heidegger's withdrawn

tool-system, or even a formless pre-Socratic *apeiron*. There is another sort of philosophy that permits no existence of anything hidden, as in Berkeley's ideas without underlying material, Hegel's collapse of the noumenal into the movement of negativity, Husserl's immanent phenomena, and Latour's actors without hidden residue. But the perennial question of whether or not there is an unbridgeable gap between thought and world is, we have seen, a subordinate dispute that conceals a wider agreement on the twofold onto-taxonomy of thought and world. Although OOO is more sympathetic to the first of the two groups, that is not the point: even a "realism" or "materialism" that considers the real solely as a contrast to human thought remains a form of onto-taxonomy. The traumatic Lacanian Real, as championed by Žižek, is an especially good example.[18]

A more interesting question concerns the subject on top of the world. Of course there is widespread awareness that we cannot speak of an isolated subject apart from the world, that the individual is always embedded in a wider movement of history and culture, of intersubjectivity, or of embodiment. But what is generally missed is that even the individual subject is an *object* when viewed from the outside, and not in the bad sense that someone is unfairly "objectified" by others. More precisely, what is missed is that human absorption with something or someone—which is usually called "intentionality," but might also be given the Dantean-Schelerian name of *love*—is not just a tense balancing act between separate object and subject poles, but a compound object in its own right. We feel fear and pity toward the loves of others in tragedy, or laugh at those "worse than we are" (Aristotle) in comedy.[19] We can even be enthralled by the cynicism of those who mock or berate the objects of their own "ironic" concern; in the end, such irony is just a privative version of sincerity, no different in kind from straightforward pity, laughter, or hatred. From our own point of view it might seem that we "transcend" the objects of our concern, but we do not really transcend them at all. Instead, our intentional relation to an object can itself be considered as an object—one no different in kind from Oedipus, Beatrice, carbon, an automobile, or quarks. This happens when others reflect on our relations to objects, and already when we reflect on these relations ourselves. But this means that far from being at the top of the cosmos, the subject is positioned in a permanent mezzanine level, with a chain of further objects reaching indefinitely upward and downward alike. This means that the subject can always be found on the interior of some wider object to which it belongs, and is not some unique point of transcendence or negativity that rises above everything else.

Although deconstruction has trained two generations of critics to express an almost robotic disdain for the "metaphysical" character of such terms as "inside" and "outside," these words have perfectly innocent meanings that are useful for our purposes. Consider the case of Dante's love for Beatrice, whether it be for the historical Bice di Folco Portinari (as in *La vita nuova*) or for the character in the *Comedy* heavily based on her. Here it is no longer the modern schema of the subject Dante and the object Beatrice, or even a possible feminist reversal in which she is the subject and Dante the object of her gaze in return. Instead, we have a more compounded structure that is simply foreign to modern philosophy's outlook. Let's take it first from Dante's perspective, since we are more familiar with him due to his direct authorial voice. Dante the amorous agent is a *real object*: not just a transcendental subject gazing upon a pictorial scene, but someone who deploys his reality in loving and hating some objects rather than others. Consider his love for Beatrice. Husserl would tell us that Beatrice is Dante's intentional object; as such she also differs from her qualities, since these shift constantly as she is viewed from alternative angles and in differing clothing and moods. Since the word "intentional" often leads to confusion over whether it refers to an object inside the mind (Franz Brentano) or outside it

(Husserl), OOO replaces it with the term "sensual."[20] This yields the pair of Beatrice as *sensual object* and the flickering adumbrations of her *sensual qualities* that change constantly from one moment to the next. Please note that the term is "sensual," not "sensible": we are not referring to Beatrice as an object of the senses as opposed to an object of the mind or of practical activity, both of which—in OOO terms—are every bit as sensual as sense experience itself. "Sensual" covers anything that exists in relation, whether it be fully conceptual experience or unnoticed causal interaction. Now, Husserl maintains further that the phenomenologist is able to intuit the true qualities of Beatrice, the ones that belong to her no matter what specific profile she presents to Dante's view. Such intuition, Husserl contends, occurs through the intellect rather than through the senses. For OOO, these true qualities of Beatrice are called *real* qualities, and they lie beyond both Dante's love for her and Husserl's intellectual intuition of her, no matter how hard they both try. And apart from these qualities, Beatrice is also an inaccessible and unified *real object* lying beyond any relation to her, of whatever sort that relation may be.

On the interior of this *amour*, this intentional relation, what we now have is Dante as real object absorbed with Beatrice as a rift between *sensual object* and *sensual qualities*. Of course he never experiences Beatrice in a vacuum, but always in a medium populated with countless other sensual objects and qualities, though we must leave these complexities for another occasion. This medium, for which I will introduce the term "cell," contains three basic elements: the *real object* (Dante) absorbed by what it confronts and the *sensual object and qualities* (of Beatrice) with which the real object Dante is absorbed. The real object Beatrice and her real qualities lie outside the cell, since by definition they are inexhaustible in any given encounter. Dante the amorous agent or real object also has *real qualities*, though they also lie outside the cell. As a reminder, we can also take Beatrice as agent rather than patient, in which case the roles are reversed: now we have Beatrice as the real object whose real qualities are left outside the cell, while the Dante she observes becomes a rift between sensual objects and qualities whose real counterparts are stranded outside the relation. But note that these are *two different objects* despite their mutual dependence. In the first case the compound is made up of real Dante and sensual Beatrice, and in the second it is precisely reversed. But not all relations are necessarily mutual like this one: we can also be absorbed with distant or ancient objects that do not encounter us in return, as happens with the numerous long-dead stars in the nighttime sky.

Yet there is another "outside" in this situation that has nothing to do with the hidden Beatrice who is a surplus deeper than however she is encountered: I speak of that which is *above* the interior rather than below it. That is to say, in the case where Dante is the agent, his absorption with Beatrice can in turn become an object for someone or something else—and even for himself. Abundant examples occur in *La vita nuova*, where the friends of Bice notice Dante's love for their friend and make numerous teasing, fearful, or tragic remarks about it. The same holds for readers who spend their hours with Dante's writings, for the birds who recoil from this agitated lover in the streets of medieval Florence, and even for the atmosphere that slowly absorbs the additional carbon dioxide emitted by his labored breath. Borrowing from the social systems theory of Luhmann, we might call this the "environment" that is excluded for now from the Dante–Beatrice system.[21]

We need a name for the interior of any compound object, and I see no better option than the biological term "cell," which—ironically enough—came to biology from architecture. This choice is inspired by the work of the Chilean immunologists Maturana and Varela, whose influence on Continental theory far predates my own interest in them.[22] Their initial concern was with the dynamics of the biological cell, which they describe as a *homeostatic* function: one that works primarily to maintain a steady internal state. The outside world is irrelevant except insofar as it can be processed in terms meaningful to the interior of the cell. In this way, they make use of a simple distinction between the system of the cell and its environment. But OOO adds important additional features to the picture. For one thing, the inner/outer model is converted into a fourfold structure consisting of rifts between object/quality and real/sensual, a purely philosophical issue that does not cross the immunologists' radar. For another, these Chileans do not give much consideration to further inner/outer relations that occur within the cell itself. That is to say, the various cell organelles do not just participate in the cellular system, but should also be treated as autonomous realities not fully exhausted by the life of the cell as a whole. This means that there are other hidden "environments" within the internal parts of the cell along with the surrounding one in the world outside. Finally, Maturana and Varela are often accused—rightly, in my view—of offering too little guidance as to how the cell does gain *indirect* access to the outside world. This problem is emphasized nicely by the authorial team of Dunham, Grant, and Watson, who report that Maturana and Varela's "account of organizational closure, and the complete specification of structural modulation by the organization, [is] overplayed. This results in, at best, Kantian or phenomenological constructivism, and, at worst, complete nihilistic solipsism."[23] There is the additional difficulty that, since Maturana and Varela are scientists after all, they do not wish to treat the cell system as completely closed off from their own knowledge of it. As the aforementioned commentators put it: "Like Hegel, and unlike Kant, Maturana and Varela are quite convinced of the capacity of the human intellect, in principle, to grasp the autopoietic reality of life."[24] More than this, they "mock the suggestion that life is impervious to our intellect."[25] Dunham and colleagues observe that the Chileans try to bridge the gap between these opposed poles of knowledge and closure by arguing that "there is no representation in cognition. Neither we, nor any other organism, extract information from a pre-given world and 'represent' it to ourselves. . . . Cognition, then, is not *of* a world; rather . . . cognition '*brings forth a world.*'"[26] While the mechanisms of this solution might seem obscure, we will see that it is basically on the right track.

With this model of the cell, we have fully abandoned the topography of the world adopted by modern philosophy.[27] Instead of thought on top and world (whether noumenal or phenomenal) on the bottom, we now have the following, more intricate picture. There is most definitely a world beneath the cell, but not at some ultimate rock bottom of reality: the entities that exceed intentional experience are themselves further compounds, each with its own interior, and there is no compelling reason to expect some final underlying layer. As for thought—in the widest sense, which includes perceiving and using—it too is an object that forms a cell closed off from the other objects that encounter it. But whereas the layers may descend downward infinitely, this is not the case with upward movement. For while every intention is haunted by other real objects eluding it below, it is not the case that every compound is necessarily embedded in higher ones.[28] That is to say, there is no reason to hold—with the philosopher Jonathan Schaeffer and others—that there must be some all-encompassing object called "the world."[29] Reality extends downward without limit, but ends somewhere above in a shifting, raggedy roofline.

An additional point should be made about this cellular model of reality, whose original model is the windowless monad of Leibniz.[30] The idea of an autonomous worldly substance begins with Aristotle, one of the titans of Western philosophy, whose contributions have been momentarily trivialized in the antirealist atmosphere of recent decades. In the words of Julián Marías, "Whenever philosophy has established *real* contact with Aristotle, it has immediately become more precise and serious."[31] Leibniz adds two important dimensions to the Aristotelian tradition. First, he recognizes that the autonomy of individual substances raises the important question of how two autonomous things could possibly interact. Although his solution—that they interact by way of God's "pre-established harmony"—cannot help us today, the problem itself remains of decisive importance. Second, Leibniz places all experience on the interior of monads, whereas for Aristotle nothing really happens "inside" a substance. As seen from the cellular theory sketched here, all experience occurs on the inside of an object for OOO as well, giving Leibniz the status of a crucial precedent. But the main point I wish to add is that when it comes to the cell, there are two types of mediation going on, which we can term the *medium* and the *mediator*. First, there is the background medium provided by any situation, where we operate in largely unconscious fashion. But second, in any situation we also find one or more mediators that allow us passage into situations beyond the current one. The difference between these is sufficiently important that it has not gone unnoticed by previous thinkers. Marshall McLuhan devoted his career to studying the unconscious background effects of all media, but he also had an underrated theory of why a medium eventually collapses in favor of a new one, along the opposite paths of "reversal" and "retrieval."[32] Roland Barthes's *Camera Lucida* gives us an analogous theory of photography, in which the medium of any given photograph (or *studium*) sets a general tone and mood, while a single element (or *punctum*) grabs the beholder's attention and guides the experience. More recently, Badiou's philosophy contrasts the mediocrity of given "situations" or "worlds" with the "evental traces" that enable us to experience "truths" that go well beyond the current situation.[33] The OOO way of accounting for this duality is through a contrast between literal and nonliteral (or "aesthetic") experience, to which we now turn. Before doing so, we might note in passing that architecture has these same two dimensions, largely coinciding with the difference between the internal space and the façade or exterior surface of a building.

The Root Problem of Literalism

We have just mentioned Leibniz's underrated problem: if reality is made up of enclosed and disconnected cells, then what is the mechanism by which these cells form links with each other? It is here that the fundamental role of aesthetics comes into play. Among the numerous defects of modern philosophy is an excessive commitment to *literalism.* The literalist position holds that whether or not the world exists beyond human access, we can adequately deal with it by properly ascribing qualities to objects. And indeed, it is entirely possible to make more or less accurate literal propositions about objects, which we all do on a regular basis: this is what we call *knowledge,* and modernity is nothing if not obsessed with knowledge. Science rules the age, with the arts and humanities treated as soft and secondary—though the social sciences try hard to be as exact as the natural ones, and philosophy in its analytic branch bases its entire claim to legitimacy on a mimicry of scientific culture. The problems with this approach have not gone unnoticed, and there have been numerous worthy efforts to account for nonliteral forms of cognition. Kant tried this early on with his "regulative ideas" in ontology about such entities as God and the universe, which cannot be known directly but still serve to guide us in life. He tried it again in his ethics, in which we must assume our human freedom even though our actions are presumably subject to the same causal laws as inanimate matter. Yet Kant's best such effort was surely his conception of "taste" in the Third Critique, which refers to aesthetic cognition that cannot be paraphrased in conceptual language. Heidegger's forays into poetic language make much the same effort, even if they are widely mocked in rationalist circles as an effort to let "bad poetry" dethrone the admirable rigors of knowledge.[34] But even in the philosophy of science there have been impressive challenges to the literalist model, whether in the fallibilism of Popper and Lakatos or in the paradigm-based model of revolution in Thomas Kuhn.[35]

Rationalism is above all a literalist enterprise, and this means a business devoted to *accurate propositional content.* Even in Continental philosophy rationalism now rules the age, as seen in the popularity of Meillassoux and Brassier in certain circles.[36] Yet there is good reason to question the literalist conception. If Heidegger is not to one's liking, there are more venerable sources, such as Aristotle's *Rhetoric,* focused as it is on the crucial role of the "enthymeme" that eludes explicit formulation. There is also McLuhan's career-long argument that the background effects of any medium are of greater significance than their consciously noticed contents.[37] In the arts there is Greenberg, undeservedly out of fashion for fifty years, who argues that modernist painting must come to terms with the flat canvas background rather than the pictorial content of painting. All these thinkers draw our attention to what lies *behind* any explicit content. But we can also escape literalism in the other direction, as soon as we notice that one and the same content can be presented in numerous different modes. J. L. Austin's influential speech act theory makes a key distinction between "constative" or literal speech on the one hand and "performative" speech that commits us to what we are saying on the other, even though the two modes can be identical as to content.[38] Badiou argues that there is no event without the subject's *fidelity* to it, and claims further that philosophy is shadowed by an "anti-philosophical" tradition in which content is subordinate to a sort of primal, subrational "experience that does not deceive"—as in Pascal, Kierkegaard, Nietzsche, Wittgenstein, Lacan, and ultimately Badiou himself.[39] Combining both sides of Badiou in advance is Socrates, the real founder of Western philosophy, whose practice of *philosophia* is aware not only of the inaccessibility of truth to adequate definition (subcontent) but also of the parallel need for philosophy as a way of life (supercontent).

With its new distinctions between real/sensual and objects/qualities, OOO provides fresh technical equipment for showing why literalism fails. Let's take the case of oxygen and our knowledge about it. Oxygen has the atomic number 8, which means that it has eight protons in its nucleus. Since it normally occurs on our planet in the form of dioxygen (O_2), it has an atomic mass of 15.999, or nearly double its atomic number. These facts help explain oxygen in terms of its components (undermining). But we can also move in the other direction and speak of how it relates to its environment (overmining). On the Celsius scale, oxygen melts at −218.79 and boils at −182.962, giving it a rather narrow and frigid window as a liquid. In its gaseous form on earth, oxygen is traversed by sound at a speed of 330 meters per second. In whichever direction we move, downward or upward, oxygen can be described by true and measurable qualities. Assuming an infinite period of research, we might well learn literally everything there is to know about oxygen, even if in practice there are infinitely many relations between it and other things that might be studied without end. In short, the object called oxygen is treated as a "bundle of qualities" (Hume) that can in principle be fully discerned, even if at any point in time the bundle has not yet been fully assessed.[40] In the case of oxygen, as with other objects studied by the natural sciences, it might be difficult to imagine what other secrets, or not-yet-discovered qualities, it holds in store: implicit traits that could eventually be made explicit with a bit of work.[41] Stated differently, it might be argued that there is only a "quantitative" excess in things and not a "qualitative" one, as Peter Wolfendale claims in his pugnacious critique of OOO.[42]

But now let's imagine a poem about oxygen. While this might sound less appealing than odes to waterfowl or lovers, a hymn to oxygen is at least conceivable. And more than conceivable: at the very moment of writing these words I have searched online and found a poem titled "An Element Called Oxygen," written by an author using the pen name Aztlanquill, which begins with the following two lines:

An Element called oxygen; of you I shall breathe 'til
  dead,
when my lungs implode and lie in a silent spread.

The whole of the poem is not lacking in competence and a certain charm. Clearly it does not aspire to science or literal statement: it is a poem, after all. It provides no information about the deep structure of the eighth chemical element, though it does go on to give some examples of its relational effects. If we try to paraphrase the poem in the manner of a student subjected to a compulsory schoolhouse exercise, it might go something like this: "Basically, 'An Element Called Oxygen' says that people have to breathe oxygen all their lives until they die. It is part of the atmosphere, invisible, and increases due to the activity of plants, but also in other ways." Now, anyone with the least aesthetic sensitivity would recognize this as a poor reading indeed. The poem's penultimate line, for instance, tells us roughly that oxygen is fed by all plant life on the earth, including trees. Can we really paraphrase this line as saying that oxygen "increases due to the activity of plants"? We would do so only if we were engaging in deliberate mockery. What happens instead in the poem is that the oxygen seems to come to life. Oxygen is *fed*, suggesting a ravenous appetite on the part of this inanimate chemical. It is fed in part not just by trees, but by *all* trees, hinting at a vast arboreal conspiracy. Moreover, it is not just all trees, but all trees *from the earth*, which also brings soil and bedrock into the cartel. Even if we insist that this is merely improper personification of an inanimate chemical, the poem still does genuine cognitive work. By ascribing so much unfamiliar drama to the life of oxygen, the line in question splits oxygen as an inscrutable *object* from oxygen as a *bundle of qualities*: whether those that science measures in mathematizable form or those that practical life uses as it will. In OOO terms, the poem produces an object/quality rift, which is precisely what theoretical knowledge and practical know-how equally avoid.

What happens in such cases is that a given object in the poem acquires qualities that are too unfamiliar to be experienced literally, as with oxygen and the trope of its being "fed." The qualities remain accessible on the surface—since we already have a good banal sense of what "fed" means— yet an oxygen-object that eats is unfamiliar to us. While the oxygen of literal statement is a *sensual* object suggesting no inaccessible depth, the oxygen that would be fed is a mysterious *real* one. But real objects are by definition unapproachable. And since phenomenology has shown (to my satisfaction, at least) that there are no qualities that do not adhere to some underlying object, we know that "fed" must belong to some object. But it cannot be the sensual oxygen, because then we would remain at the level of sensual experience and would simply be making literal statements—which, by hypothesis, is not the case here. The oxygen of the poem must instead be an inaccessible *real* object, since otherwise the magic of aesthetic experience would never occur. And since the real object oxygen is absent by definition, and must therefore be ruled out as the bearer of "fed" qualities, there is only one remaining option: the only real object that never withdraws from the cell is the beholder. That is to say, I *myself* perform the oxygen and experience its quality of being fed by all trees from the earth. It is the old concept of *mimesis,* but completely reversed: namely, it is not that the artist manufactures imitations of objects, but that the beholder of art *enacts* a nonliteral imitation of what is beheld.[43] This is enough to clarify why aesthetic experience deploys our entire being, whereas literal statements do not draw us into their midst as anything more than neutral beholders who agree or disagree with their content, with the latter operation making up the entire mental life of dogmatic rationalists.

Returning to Dunham, Grant, and Watson's interpretation of Maturana and Varela, we now see that the immunologists were speaking of something very much like aesthetic experience as the root of all change: "There is no representation in cognition. Neither we, nor any other organism, extract information from a pre-given world and 'represent' it to ourselves. . . . Cognition, then, is not *of* a world; rather . . . cognition '*brings forth a world.*'"[44] Assuming that we are actually absorbed by the oxygen poem rather than bored by it, the poem "brings forth a world" in this way. A nonliteral approach to philosophy entails that, rather than representing the world in constative fashion, we "bring it forth" in performative manner. Aesthetics is explosive. We can no more remove it from the universe for rationalism's sake than we can flatten a globe onto a two-dimensional map without distorting the size and shape of its land masses. Since rationalism is a literalism, rationalism is wrong; it simply dismisses an important dimension of reality for its own convenience. Whereas rationalism knows only sensual objects and hunts for the appropriate sensual-measurable qualities that belong to them, OOO is also concerned with the crossing of real objects and sensual qualities.

Whenever the nonconceptual character of art for Kant is mentioned, discussion turns too quickly to "the sublime," by which he means what is *absolutely* large or powerful by contrast with the human scale.[45] But it is hardly necessary to appeal straightaway to the sublime: as Jacques Rancière astutely notes, Kantian *beauty* is already beyond all paraphrase.[46] No one can explain what makes a particular rose beautiful; this can be experienced only through taste. Nor can anyone give a list of rules for how to produce beautiful things, as Greenberg reminds us again in *Homemade Esthetics.*[47] The beautiful object is cut off from everything else: from all interest and agreeableness, and ultimately from the whole of its sociopolitical or biographical context. This is what makes Kant a formalist. But in the end, his position is an exaggeration in several ways. One is shown by Bloom when he demonstrates that literary works always emerge as a challenge to earlier works; another is that we know it is perfectly possible for a great poem to have profound socio-political ramifications. Yet we should not overlook the fact that, despite his exaggerations, Kant is basically correct. A poem makes contact with some but not all predecessor poems, and critics can work out these influences with vary-ing degrees of success. A painting may spark a revolution or break the heart of a queen, but it does not simultaneously affect everything else in the universe. An artwork relates to some things but not others, and in relating to those partic-ular things, it brings them into its cell while leaving the rest outside. Relations take work, and the vast majority of possi-ble relations simply never occur. This is why many or most readings of literary works fail badly, and why not every work is fully penetrable by Marxism, psychoanalysis, or any other interpretive school.

Cut off from its surroundings, the beautiful object achieves what Kant calls *pure* beauty. But what about architecture, which for Kant can never be pure, since there is always some sort of utility involved? We recall that Kant's central mis-take was to adopt too *narrow* a formalism in which the sole required separation is that between beholder and object. Hav-ing established the model of the cell—or even having simply read Fried's work on Manet—we can see that the cell always contains a theatrical relationship in which the beholder is dramatically absorbed in the object.[48] Jean Baudrillard has theorized this relation brilliantly under the term "seduc-tion."[49] But if even a visual artwork is hopelessly entangled with its beholder, then it is not a special case of pure and uncontaminated beauty that would make architecture deriv-ative by contrast. If an artwork ejects its object pole into the inaccessible real beyond, and thus turns the beholder into a real object performing the work's leftover sensual qualities, we will see that architecture simply does this by more complicated means. Architecture, being professionally unable to exclude all relations in principle, is better equipped than art to understand that relations are not a mortal threat to autonomy, as long as we find a new way to consider them. Moreover, Kant should have known this better than anyone else. When he famously speaks of beauty as "purposiveness without purpose," he means to exclude architecture among other things (a human body, a horse) while failing to recognize that architecture is already about purposiveness rather than purpose.[50] The remainder of this book aims to develop the consequences.

This has been a somewhat compressed and difficult chapter, one whose links with architecture might not yet be clear. But we needed to establish the following points, bulleted here for the reader's convenience:

- Autonomy and formalism are necessary concepts. Otherwise, one falls too easily into the promiscuous holism of "everything communicates with everything else" and may leap to improper conclusions about the communicative powers of a nonexistent *Zeitgeist.*
- Autonomy and formalism do not mean that everything is completely self-contained, only that every link requires work and demands payment.
- Every version of formalism excludes certain relations while permitting others. Kant's own version is too narrowly obsessed with preventing the specific relation between beholder and artwork.
- Against Kant's assumption, the relation between beholder and artwork is the backbone of all art, as Fried himself came to realize in his later works.
- Yet the artwork remains autonomous, since the relation between beholder and work is still cut off from everything else, unless additional work is done to forge links.

- Since the visual artwork is already "impure" due to the relational structure at its core, there is nothing disqualifying about the impure status of architecture in the Kantian framework. The added relational elements of architecture make it slightly more exotic from a formalist standpoint, but this is a speculative opportunity rather than a defect.

- The visual artwork already consists of a central relation cut off from all other relations, but architecture is forced to confront this duel of relation and nonrelation head-on, in a way that visual art is not.

- Literalism sees no difference between the object and the bundle of qualities through which it is known. All knowledge is literal, since it reduces objects either downward to the qualities of its pieces or upward to the qualities of its effects and knows no way of meeting the object on its own terms. Duchamp can certainly place a literal object in an arts context, but in doing so he has already deliteralized it. The literal and the aesthetic are opposites. A thing appears either as a bundle of qualities or as a rift between object and qualities. This difference cannot be deconstructed, and hence Derrida is wrong to claim there is no such thing as literal language.[51]

- Aesthetic experience, like all experience, has the structure of a cell. Beneath it are inscrutable realities that must be addressed indirectly rather than literally. Above it are the wider and more complex realities into which it enters. Reality can intrude upon the cell from either side.

- Within the cell of aesthetic experience, sensual objects are torn between their unified objecthood and their plurality of features. What makes an experience aesthetic is that the beholder stands in for the withdrawn unity of the aesthetic object while holding together its qualities. This is why all art is theatrical, architecture included.

5 THE ARCHITECTURAL CELL

ANYONE WRITING A BOOK ON THE 1800S COULD DO MUCH worse than choosing the title *A Century of Historicism*. With Hegel, philosophy internalized history by treating it as a series of dialectical approaches to truth rather than a sequence of abandoned logical blunders.[1] The study of history itself made a great leap forward with the insightful work of Wilhelm Dilthey, among others.[2] With Charles Darwin's theory of natural selection, humans and all other species became deeply historical rather than immutable archetypes.[3] Earlier, in the pioneering work of Charles Lyell, the apparently stable features of the present-day earth were shown to be transient outcomes of an ongoing play of forces, and thus the new science of geology was born.[4] Archaeology took on modern form toward century's end as well, most famously with Heinrich Schliemann's work at the site of ancient Troy.

In the same period, architecture was awash in a revival of historical styles, as seen in the Beaux-Arts tradition that modernism aimed to replace. There was also intense fascination with the Gothic in Britain, France, and Germany alike, with each of these nations laying claim to the style as somehow uniquely its own, though France is usually considered the winner of the prize: the Abbey of Saint-Denis, reworked from the 1130s under the direction of the celebrated Abbot Suger, is taken to be the original impetus for the Gothic building trend.[5] Early in the nineteenth century, the German writer Joseph Görres lobbied for the completion of the unfinished medieval Cologne Cathedral; although this work did not resume until decades later, the final result was one of the great monuments of Gothic architecture, completed well after the period to which it belongs.[6] In Britain we find the fanatical Catholic convert A. W. N. Pugin making a case for Gothic as not just historically great but also more technically excellent than contemporary styles, as in his 1841 book *The True Principles of Pointed or Christian Architecture*. Perhaps most important, in France there was the major theorist Eugène-Emmanuel Viollet-le-Duc, who saw Gothic as more "rational" than later European traditions, thereby building a bridge from Gothic to modernism.[7] Yet there were numerous other historically based trends during the century, many of them not guided by a spirit of rationalism at all. There is a case to be made that modernism gained steam primarily through a gradual loss of appetite for the historical and ornamental spirit of the preceding century, including the negative modernist reaction to the ornate *art nouveau* and *Jugendstil* currents at the beginning of the twentieth century.

In any case, we have already reviewed Sullivan's functionalist maxim that "form ever follows function," and have shown its innovative position with respect to Kantian aesthetics. Rather than downplaying the usefulness of architecture, Sullivan treats function as the *root* of form, so that the two gain a new joint purity by excluding all considerations ulterior to a building's purpose. If Chicago in the 1880s was the breeding ground for numerous innovations on this front, including the emergence of the great skyscraper that became America's national emblem, it was also Chicago in 1893 that plunged

American architecture back into European historicism. In that year Sullivan's career went into terminal decline following the famed World's Columbian Exposition in Chicago, a wonderland of Beaux-Arts style that reawakened historicist tastes across the nation, mirrored in Rand's *The Fountainhead* in the mental breakdown of the fictional Henry Cameron. Thereafter it was Sullivan's former employee Frank Lloyd Wright who became most closely associated with modernism in America. Wright's status in architecture today is unusual, and worth a few words in passing. If we ask a random person on the street to name a famous scientist, they are likely to say Albert Einstein; ask the same person for a famous architect, and they will probably name Wright, at least in the United States. One of my students at SCI-Arc was told by an Uber driver that Wright was the greatest architect of all time—at the very instant they were passing a fresh Los Angeles masterpiece by Gehry! Nevertheless, one of the surprises that awaited me as a newcomer to the field was just how seldom Wright's name comes up in architectural conversation. He remains revered in the Taliesin circles devoted to his legacy, but these circles are themselves rather marginalized in mainstream discourse. This is certainly not due to any contempt for his work. When I asked one colleague about Wright's absence from discussion, he answered that Wright works too much in a "vernacular" spirit: the architectural term for building from regional tradition rather than worked-out theoretical principles. Gage puts it more bluntly in his polemic with Schumacher, drawing an analogy between Wright and the late Zaha Hadid. When Schumacher proposes "parametricism"—an attempted theorization of Hadid's work and his own—as a potentially dominant style for the future of architecture, Gage predicts a rather different fate for this school:

> Schumacher's references to Parametricism replacing both Le Corbusier's *Vers une architecture* and the International Style are the wrong historical model. I would suggest that the gorgeous fluid signature of Hadid, being so recognizably

her own, is much closer to a historical model of Frank Lloyd Wright—an absolute master whose signature is so author-specific as to be nearly untouchable by other architects. In this light, Schumacherian Parametricism is destined not to become the next great global style as much as the new Taliesin—a school of thought with very few, but very dedicated—nay, fanatical—believers content to rehearse old architectural scripts well beyond their expiration date.[8]

One need not agree with Gage's assessment of Hadid, Schumacher, or parametricism to gain an important insight from this passage. When Gage refers to Wright as an "absolute master" whose style is "nearly untouchable," this somehow strikes the mark. Wright is viewed less as the founder of a movement with improvable principles than as a one-man birth and culmination who can have no heirs, only initiates. This helps explain why American supporters of high modern architecture in the 1920s and 1930s were always uneasy with Wright. As early as 1929, Henry-Russell Hitchcock argued for two separate categories of modernists, with the first of them treated as inferior: this "New Tradition" included such figures as Wagner in Vienna and Wright himself, while the more favorable term "New Pioneers" referred to such now-canonical modernists as Le Corbusier and the Bauhaus directors Walter Gropius and Mies.[9] Wright made vigorous retort to Hitchcock the following year:

> Most new "modernistic" houses manage to look as though cut from cardboard with scissors, the sheets of cardboard folded or bent in rectangles with an occasional curved cardboard surface added to get relief. The cardboard forms thus made are glued together in box-like forms—in a childish attempt to make buildings resemble steamships, flying machines, or locomotives. . . . Of late, they are the superficial, badly built product of this superficial, new "surface-and-mass" aesthetic falsely claiming French painting as a parent.[10]

It is fair to say that Wright's counterattack failed to hit home in circles beyond his immediate devotees. The main current of modern architecture instead followed the path of Le Corbusier, Gropius, and Mies, as theorized by their court intellectual, Giedion.[11]

Le Corbusier, born in Francophone Switzerland in 1887 under the name Charles-Édouard Jeanneret, has a good claim to be called the Picasso of modern architecture. When in 2017 the Pritzker Prize winner Thom Mayne asked a distinguished panel of architects to list one hundred essential buildings from the period 1900 to 2000, Le Corbusier led the way with eight mentions, including the top two on the list (the 1931 Villa Savoye and the 1955 Chapelle Notre-Dame du Haut).[12] He was trailed by Mies with six buildings, Wright (who straddled two centuries) with five, Louis Kahn with four, and Alvar Aalto and Carlo Scarpa with three apiece. But the parallel between Corb and Picasso bears on more than their prominent reputations. In spite of Wright's remark

Le Corbusier, Villa Savoye, Poissy, France. Photograph by Margaret Griffin.

that recent modernism "falsely claim[s] French painting as a parent," there is a heavily cubist influence in Corb's buildings. We will also see that he was more of a Kantian than might be expected for someone known to the public for his functionalist-sounding motto, "The house is a machine for living in."[13] In fact, I will contend that he was more of a Kantian than Sullivan was, and that the main line of modern architecture is less functionalist in spirit than the general public believes—a view not especially controversial among architects, despite Le Corbusier's ostensible use of the plan as the primary generator. On this note, let's turn first to his epoch-making book *Towards a New Architecture* (1923 in French, 1927 in English), and then to Eisenman's attempted inversion of functionalism into formalism. From there we can make a concluding statement on one of our two questions: the relation between architecture and the visual arts.

Functionalism

In *Space, Time and Architecture,* Giedion writes glowingly as follows: "So far as I can see, Le Corbusier is the only architect of our time for whom there are sufficient grounds to say that he had an all-embracing genius: as an architect, painter, and urbanist with the vision of a poet." Placing him squarely in the canon of the discipline, Giedion adds that Raphael, Michelangelo, and the Renaissance master Donato Bramante "each possessed an all-embracing genius which is renewed in Le Corbusier."[14] Another such genius, Leonardo da Vinci, made real but less significant contributions to architecture. Though one hesitates to agree with Giedion that Le Corbusier was a "genius" in painting, the breadth of his talents is obvious enough, and he is surely the prime candidate for the title of foremost architect of the twentieth century.[15] Any contrarian case made for Wright would have to reckon with the fact that his maturity began in the 1800s.

At any rate, no one has a better claim to stand at the center of modern architecture than Le Corbusier, and his *Towards a New Architecture* is essential reading for anyone interested in the field. Perhaps the most famous specific claim in the book is the aforementioned assertion that "the house is a machine for living in," a maxim repeated at least ten times despite the relative brevity of the work.[16] In philosophy this phrase is infamous among Heideggerians, who express horror at the idea by contrasting it with Heidegger's own notion of "dwelling," which—as we have seen—had a delayed effect on architecture in its own right.[17]

To refer to the house as a machine for living in sounds at first like the quintessence of functionalism. This impression is reinforced by the ink Le Corbusier spills in praise of engineers, who are described as "healthy and virile, active and useful, balanced and happy in their work," while the architects of his era are dismissed as "disillusioned and unemployed, boastful and peevish," and who come from their schools having learned "the obsequiousness of the toady" (14). We seem to have a self-hating architect on our hands, and perhaps even a self-hating European: "We have the American grain elevators and factories, the magnificent first-fruit of the new age. The American engineers overwhelm with their calculations our expiring [European] architecture" (31).[18] Today it is the engineers, not the architects, who "find themselves in accord with the principles that Bramante and Raphael had applied a long time ago" (41). While architects persist in timid academic deference to the past, "our daring and masterly constructors of steamships produce palaces in comparison with which cathedrals are tiny things" (92). In this spirit, we should seek "a house like a motor-car, conceived and carried out like an omnibus or a ship's cabin" (240). Indeed, the homely innovation of reinforced concrete is on the verge of changing our aesthetic standards altogether (63). And furthermore, we must prepare ourselves for the virtue of mass-produced housing (229). It is amusing to imagine Heidegger's dramatically anguished face if he were to read this Corbusian homage to technology.[19]

Corb's admiration for engineers finds clear expression in his aesthetic maxims. Just as one would expect from a hard-core functionalist, he suppresses the classical obsession with a building's façade in favor of the plan: "The plan is what determines everything; it is the decisive moment. A plan is not a pretty thing to be drawn, like a Madonna face; it is an austere abstraction" (48–49). Such austerity is best secured by a turn to geometry, which he hails as "the language of man" (72). Here as elsewhere, engineers have taken the lead: "The essentials of architecture lies in spheres, cones and cylinders. . . . But this geometry terrifies the architects of to-day" (39–40). More and more, his book becomes a rationalist's dream, as he praises our historical passage "from the elementary satisfactions (decoration) to the higher satisfactions (mathematics)" (139). He suggests that we "clear our minds of romantic cobwebs" (238) before informing us that the student of today wants a monk's cell, not a Gothic Oxford (260). Like every good modern rationalist, Le Corbusier stresses "things that can be known" (18, emphasis removed).

Yet he also asserts repeatedly that function is not enough. Though Le Corbusier often invites us to admire virile American solutions to practical problems, he also exclaims that "it will be a delight to talk of ARCHITECTURE after so many grain-stores, workshops, machines, and sky-scrapers. . . . The purpose of construction is to MAKE THINGS HOLD TOGETHER; of architecture TO MOVE US" (19). Any straightforward functionalist reading of Corb's work would need to grapple with the following words: "When a thing responds to a need, it is not beautiful; it satisfies all one part of our mind, the primary part, without which there is no possibility of richer satisfactions; let us recover the right order of events" (110). And even more strongly: "My house is practical. I thank you, as I might thank Railway engineers, or the Telephone service.

You have not touched my heart" (153). Before anyone intones the Corbusian maxim of the house as a machine for living in, they should consider his lament that "a chair is in no way a work of art; a chair has no soul; it is a machine for sitting in" (142). After complaining that architecture has been "lowered to the level of its utilitarian purposes," he counters that "this is construction, not architecture. Architecture only exists when there is a poetic emotion" (215).

It is here that the Kantian side of Le Corbusier emerges. Immediately after complaining that chairs are mere machines, he offers a principle that might have come straight from the *Critique of Judgment*: "Art, in a highly cultivated country, finds its means of expression in pure art, a concentrated thing free from all utilitarian motives—painting, literature, music" (142). The oft-praised engineers have their limits, and we are urged to respect "the biddings of a poetical sense peculiar to the architect" (53–54). He concludes in much the same spirit: "Obviously, if the roof were to fall in, if the central heating did not work, if the walls cracked, the joys of architecture would be greatly diminished. . . . [Yet] architecture only exists when there is a poetic emotion" (215).[20] What this suggests is a sort of inverted Sullivan: rather than form following function, we have function following the lead of poetry, which in more Kantian terms means that function follows form. As if to emphasize his debt to the Third Critique even further, Le Corbusier tells us early in the book that architecture is "capable of the sublime" (25). In an echo of the Addisonian "Great," he asserts that "there exists one thing which can ravish us, and that is measure or scale. To achieve scale!" (163). Rowe pushes this reading further, de-emphasizing the rationalist Le Corbusier all the more. In discussing Corb's Villa Stein at Garches, Rowe remarks that it does not provide "the unchallengeable clarity of Palladio's volumes. . . . It is, instead, a type of planned obscurity . . . and Le Corbusier, in spite of the comforts which mathematics affords him, simply in terms of his location in history can occupy no such unassailable position [as Palladio's resort to eternal mathematical proportion]."[21] Here, Rowe presses to the verge of a counterintuitive reading: Le Corbusier as an architect of the picturesque. If this is the case, then the consequences for the usual view of modernism are severe indeed.

Returning for now from the sublime to the beautiful, what does it take to design beauty, which Corb concedes is already a step beyond the mere convenience of engineering? In a negative sense, we have seen that a certain austerity is needed. "Art is an austere thing" (100) and occurs "when man, in nobility of aim and complete sacrifice of all that is accidental in Art, has reached the higher levels of the mind" (204). Le Corbusier appeals to reason, but in an age-old rationalist trope he calls it "cold" reason, as if any other temperature would be mere self-indulgence (109). There is also a wonderfully opinionated moment when he warns that "to send architectural students to Rome is to cripple them for life" (173). Rejecting the motley template of historical "styles," Corb advises that "surfaces [should not] become parasitical, eating up mass and absorbing it to their own advantage: the sad story of our present-day work" (37).

So much for what he refuses. In more positive terms, "the true and profound laws of architecture . . . are established on mass, rhythm, and proportion" (286). One must use elementary shapes (159), and they must be placed in precise relationships with each other (220). In historical terms, "Egyptian, Greek or Roman architecture is an architecture of prisms, cubes and cylinders, pyramids or spheres. . . . Gothic art [by contrast] is not, fundamentally, based on spheres, cones and cylinders" (29–30). He does not shy away from pointed conclusions: "It is for that reason that a cathedral is not very beautiful and that we search in it for compensations of a subjective kind outside plastic art" (30). Primitive architecture, Le Corbusier insists, emerged from the two-dimensional analogue of "square . . . hexagon . . . octagon" (69). But these shapes are merely the elements of the architect's craft: the end to be attained is that they stand in proper relationship. In one of his most famous phrases: "Architecture is nothing but ordered arrangement [of] noble prisms, seen in light" (162–63). From the same collection of elements, many different things can be made, for in each case "there is a variation in the quality of the features and in the relationship which unites them" (203).

Perhaps the best-known example of a modern architectural masterpiece describable as an ordered arrangement of basic shapes is Utzon's Sydney Opera House. Admittedly, the shell-like components of this popular edifice are not basic Platonic masses. The official website for the building tells us that

> between 1958 and 1962, the roof design for the Sydney Opera House evolved through various iterations as Utzon and his team pursued parabolic, ellipsoid and finally spherical geometry to derive the final form of the shells. The eventual realisation that the form of the Sydney Opera House's shells could be derived from the surface of a sphere marked a milestone in 20th century architecture.[22]

But whatever the case in mathematical terms, the typical visitor to Sydney is unlikely to experience the shells as even remotely spherical. The more important point is that they are distinctly memorable, and ordered in a way that is slightly unusual and slightly asymmetrical. This recalls what the great detective novelist Raymond Chandler once said about book titles: "I have peculiar ideas about titles. They should be rather indirect and neutral, but the form of words should be a little unusual."[23] Although Chandler admits in the same letter that he failed in the case of his title *The Little Sister*, he followed the method perfectly with *The Big Sleep* and *Farewell, My Lovely*, titles composed with nothing but simple and familiar words, though in slightly unusual combinations rarely if ever used in English before. So it is with the Sydney Opera House. While there is nothing especially compelling about any of the shells taken in isolation, their ordered arrangement in a nonobvious manner combines simplicity of shape with an alluring syntax that defies easy formulation in rules. If the Opera House had been designed as a single large shell, we would have something like minimalism, and a great deal of weight would have been placed on the unified shape and the beholder's relationship with it. But due to the intriguing combination of shells, there is too much activity by the independent modules for any holism to be possible; each element seems to have a role or mission all its own, despite its obvious similarity to the other elements. This helps to counter one of the traditional dangers of formalism in literature and the visual arts, in which so much energy is spent in fending off the outside world that too little attention is paid to the autonomy of the individual aesthetic elements. In Sydney, however, the surface drama of the shells is sufficiently complex that it cannot be outweighed by any invisible background (Greenberg). There is no "planned obscurity" in the Opera House, and shifting from Utzon back to Corb, it is doubtful—contra Rowe—that there is any planned or unplanned obscurity in the latter. Le Corbusier does counter functional engineering with an appeal to beauty, but his is no beauty of the *je ne sais quoi.* Our eye quickly masters the shapes of Utzon's Sydney shells, but never quite masters their arrangement. Repeating a distinction I once made in the case of Lovecraft's writing, along with the vertical beauty that seduces us with the unknown, there is a horizontal beauty that lures us with the puzzling permutations of known elements.[24] Le Corbusier, much like Picasso, is a devotee of this latter sort of beauty; neither has an English gardener's bone in his body.

Formalism

The term "postmodernism" is notably blurry in most of the fields where it occurs. In architecture the word has a more precise sense, though even here it is a dual one, polarized between open historical quotation on one side and Deconstructivist subversion on the other. What unites the two sides is that both are still haunted by the specter of functionalism. In the words of the historian Hanno-Walter Kruft: "'Post-Modernism' signifies nothing more than a series of heterogeneous attempts to break loose from the functionalist grip." Kruft goes on to heap especial scorn on the neohistoricist branch for "lack[ing] firm intellectual foundations" and claims further that like all historically based styles, it will end up feeding once more at the functionalist trough.[25] Whether or not this is generally true, there is a more explicit philosophical effort to confront functionalism on the Deconstructivist side of postmodernism, especially in the case of Eisenman. Among the most influential figures in the field for the past half century, Eisenman represents a specific brand of formalism that implicitly offers a new response to the philosophical dilemma of architecture since Kant. In my book *Art and Objects* Fried (born 1939) was a key point of orientation, and since the slightly older Eisenman (born 1932) is of comparable stature in his own field, he can be summoned to play a similar role here.

The first thing a member of the American public usually learns about Eisenman, other than his role as designer of the Arizona Cardinals' football stadium, is probably his opposition to functionalism. In an essay first published in 1978, he laments the continued influence of those who "conceive of . . . functionalism itself as a basic theoretical proposition in architecture" (85).[26] As he sees it, the form/function opposition is not needed in architecture at all (86). Something like function began to prevail over form at the time of the Industrial Revolution, when architecture became a mass art tasked with serving various social functions (84). As a result, functionalism eventually took on the character of a moral (or even political) imperative that hijacks any internal architectural pressure on the development of form (85).

Despite its air of futuristic novelty, Eisenman contends that modern functionalism is actually rather conservative (211). If we consider his general peer group of significant architects of the past fifty years, his polar opposite in this respect would be Tschumi, despite their shared history with Derrida. In Tschumi's words: "There is no architecture without program, without action, without event. . . . Architecture is never autonomous, never pure form, and . . . architecture is not a matter of style and cannot be reduced to a language. . . . [I] aim to reinstate the term *function.*"[27] By contrast, how does Eisenman recommend that we respond to what he considers the calcifying influence of functionalism? He offers two different answers, which we might call "medium" and "spicy." Medium Eisenman concedes the necessity of function and merely denies that it should be formally emphasized: "While a house today still must shelter, it does not need to romanticize or symbolize its sheltering function; to the contrary, such symbols are today meaningless and merely nostalgic" (214), a point repeated a few years later in his open letter to Derrida.[28] Later still, he identifies this as an important cause of dispute between Alberti and his ancient forerunner: "Alberti . . . suggests that Vitruvius was stressing *firmitas* not in reference to standing up, but in reference to the *appearance* of standing up—in other words, as the sign of a structure."[29]

Spicy Eisenman is more controversial, resulting in severe critiques of some of his building practices. In this mode Eisenman not only suppresses the symbolization of function but also aims at the deliberate obstruction of functional convenience. As he tells us, in understated fashion, his Houses III and VI were "specifically developed to operate as freely as possible from functional considerations" (210). In franker terms, "several columns 'intrude on' and 'disrupt' the living and dining areas . . . [and] these 'inappropriate forms' have, according to the occupants of the house, changed the dining experience in a real and, more importantly, unpredictable fashion" (210). One would expect as much. The point of establishing such inconveniences, Eisenman reports in almost Heideggerian fashion, is to remove architecture from human control and give expression to "the *in extremis* condition under which man now lives" (218). He is admirably precise about this condition, stating that it refers specifically to the dropping of the atomic bomb in 1945: since then, for the first time in human history, none of us knows if our personal deaths will be followed by any civilization at all (170).

Here I will register three worries before moving on. (1) The claim that the form/function duality is not needed for architecture is possible only if we take "function" in the narrow sense of a distinct practical or ethical purpose. But from a OOO standpoint, since form/function has been reinterpreted more broadly as a gap between an entity's intrinsic structure and its relations with the world, this pair of terms is inescapable. A thing is what it is, but is encountered differently by other things in other situations. (2) We should ask whether the subversion of function in Houses III and VI is really the best way to bring an end to its overly central role. Heidegger's tool-analysis shows that the obtrusive character of broken equipment draws our attention to functionality all the more, even if in a privative mode.[30] (3) Although we will see that Eisenman favors volume and section over façade as a more serious site for architectural innovation, to have columns obstructing a dining area seems more like the sort of legible interruption we expect from a façade. To use the terminology introduced earlier, Houses III and VI tend to convert medium into mediator, or *studium* into *punctum*; the interior of a house becomes a façade, though one made of broken expectations rather than surfaces visible to the eye.

We have already met with Eisenman's suspicion that functionalism is ultimately a rather conservative gesture. He says this on the basis of his own, unconventional reading of architectural history. What, in the end, is modern architecture? In the late 1970s Eisenman noted that two diametrically opposite answers had recently been given to this question. At the Milan Triennale in 1973, it was proposed that modern architecture was an "outmoded functionalism" that should now make a turn toward autonomy. But at the MoMA Beaux-Arts exhibition two years later, modernism was decried as an "obsessional formalism" that should return to the functional eclecticism of the previous century. As Eisenman sees it, both extremes belong to "the 500-year-old tradition of humanism," covering the entire period from the Renaissance revival of Vitruvius up to the present (84). "Classicism . . . in imitating man through its orders and symbols, subsumed the object within the man–nature relationship" (109). The same holds for the Enlightenment, whose appeal to universal reason entailed once more "the idea that architecture's value derived from a source outside itself" (156). Sounding a lot like the early Fried, or like Meillassoux *avant la lettre,* Eisenman asserts favorably that "whereas the humanist conception aimed at an integration of subject and object, the modernist conception polemically attempt[s] their separation" (136). This puts Eisenman squarely in the mainstream of recent aesthetic formalism. While for Kant the aesthetic action all happens on the side of the human subject—though a subject taken as universal rather than individual—Greenberg and Fried flip this around: the art object itself is now the star, and the human subject demoted to a possible theatrical distraction that must limit itself to being an impassive judge of the work. In chapter 1, as in *Art and Objects,* I argued that these varying permutations of object and subject make sense only if they are seen as the two basic, unmixable drinks of the universe. No one would write that "whereas the humanist conception aimed at an integration of the colors red and blue, the modernist conception polemically attempt[s] their separation," since the difference between these two colors is clearly unworthy of occupying the foundation of the cosmos. But our minor human branch of the great apes is also not of such devastating importance that we have the power to ruin art and architecture simply by becoming too theatrically entangled with them. The human subject and nonhuman object are not such uniquely different terms in the universe that we should be especially fascinated by either their combination or their separation. Yet Eisenman is very much the modernist, and thus he takes sides, joining Greenberg and Fried in taking the "object" pole to be the more important of the two. Eisenman calls modernism "a critique of . . . man as an all-powerful, all-rational being at the center of his world" (112), failing to balance this with an equally valid critique of the "object" as a vast receptacle collecting everything that does not qualify as human. For Eisenman functionalism is a humanism, while true modernism means that "objects are . . . independent of man" (86).

This independence of the object implies two distinct kinds of autonomy: (a) autonomy for objects themselves and (b) autonomy for architecture as a discipline. Indeed, Eisenman is widely associated with the call for professional autonomy, though under Derrida's influence he eventually grew suspicious of the term. In an essay published in the late 1980s, he states: "A number of currents in modernism emphasized the autonomy of the object, seeking to abstract it from all its acculturated meanings in order to make it 'new' again" (212). So far, this sounds like vintage Eisenman. But less than ten pages later, there comes a Derridean renunciation: "The attempt at autonomy was a dream of illusory presence, of the denial of absence, of the 'other.' . . . The original goal of *autonomy*, once the source of the transformational design strategies, is no longer tenable" (221). On the same page, Eisenman abandons his previous search for "essence," "center," and "truth." In those years Derrida was at the peak of his influence, and Eisenman was not alone in being drawn away from his previous path by the charismatic Frenchman. But the critique of autonomy is not Derrida at his best, and a word is needed as to why. Eisenman grasps the central issue when he states further that *identity* must be removed from objects (187). We recall that Derrida joins

Heidegger as one of the primary critics of presence, and of the so-called metaphysics of presence or onto-theology that Heidegger was the first to condemn. Despite the air of wizardry that surrounds such phrases, the matter is not very difficult, and can be explained clearly to anyone who asks. Both terms refer, pejoratively, to the notion that reality can somehow be presented directly to the mind, whether through phenomenological reflection, scientific theorization, mathematical formalization, religious revelation, or any privileged method that claims to place the truth directly before us. While Heidegger and Derrida agree that this is impossible, their similarity ends there. For Heidegger, the best way to grasp the deficiency of presence is to consider that which is withdrawn or absent by contrast with what is explicit in any situation. Anything we encounter is merely "present-at-hand" (*vorhanden*), and this hides a vast background that can never be fully clarified; among other things, all prose statements are rooted both in historical situations and in a number of unconscious background assumptions at any given moment. But for Heidegger there is a reality hidden behind whatever is present, and this reality has a specific and definite character even though it lies forever partly beyond our reach. Derrida's version of onto-theology is more radical than Heidegger's, but to my mind less convincing. Namely, Derrida denies that presence is undercut by anything hidden, or by anything self-identical at all. As he sees it, reality is a slippery play of signs along the surface: it is not only that nothing can ever be pinned down in a specific context that reveals its true meaning, but that nothing is identical with itself in the first place. Every thing is many things; every place is many places. Indeed, Derrida's derisive term for identity is "self-presence." As he sees it, the assumption of identity, of $A = A$, of the claim that this dog is this dog and nothing else, leads us straight back into a metaphysics of presence.

The problem with Derrida's claim is simple: there are no grounds for equating identity with self-presence. For any entity, simply *to be* itself is one thing, while *to be present to itself* is quite another. The latter occurs—at most—in cases of human and perhaps higher animal introspection, and even then we do a rather poor job of making ourselves present to ourselves, which is precisely why psychotherapists stay in business. Derrida's assault on the classical principle of identity is insufficiently motivated: the turbulent life of an individual human is not the same thing as the turbulent life of a different human, a dog, or a text by Proust.[31] Everything really is itself, not everything else too. Now, an interesting question is whether Derrida realizes his difference from Heidegger on this point, or simply misreads Heidegger as agreeing with him. Eisenman seems to think—as I do—that the difference is clear enough, though he favors the Derridean version: "Derrida's idea of writing counters Heidegger's idea of being as a primary presence, as a transcendental signified, as containing a nostalgia for presence."[32] But this makes sense only if one is already convinced by Derrida that, since Heidegger's Being is identical with itself, it is ipso facto also a form of presence. If we reject Derrida's view, then it is sheer nonsense to call Heidegger a philosopher of presence, since every page of his career concerns the veiling or concealing of *Sein* from any sort of presence. Quite apart from this verdict, Eisenman seems to recognize the difference between the two philosophers better than Derrida himself. To take my favorite Derridean example, from *Of Grammatology*:

> Heidegger's insistence on noting that being is produced as history only through the logos, and is nothing outside of it, the difference between being and the entity—all this clearly indicates that fundamentally nothing escapes the movement of the signifier, and that, in the last instance, the difference between signified and signifier *is nothing*.[33]

Although philosophically daring, this summary has nothing to do with Heidegger. For the latter, Being is most definitely something more than its various configurations in the History of Being, and in no way does he deny the difference between signified and signifier. The latter point is just Yale School literary theory projected anachronistically back onto Heidegger, who in this respect is a far more classical figure. Well then, how does someone as brilliant as Derrida so badly misread a thinker whose work he knows so well? In part this can be explained through Bloom's theory of the anxiety of influence, according to which deliberate misreadings or exaggerations of a predecessor are the usual path toward one's own originality. But I have a more specific philosophical source in mind. If there is one philosopher who most strongly links identity with self-presence, it is Hegel, through his famous doctrine that "substance is subject." Stated differently, reality itself for Hegel is involved in a process of coming to self-awareness, and there is no pregiven identity apart from this process; Derrida's debt to this aspect of Hegel is perhaps clearest in his essay "*Ousia* and *Gramme.*"

In any case, there is no question that Derrida's critique of identity has palpable consequences for Eisenman's own work. For as the architect tells us, "A thing . . . is not the thing itself" (207), "the object is no longer identical to a substance" (231), and "word and thing are never one but are enfolded . . . in an original difference."[34] When he adds that rather than being a substance the object "now resides . . . in processes" (186), this muddies the waters somewhat, since process and nonidentity are not quite the same thing. But Eisenman's conclusion is firmly Derridean: "In order to be, [architecture] must always resist being" (203). To my mind, Eisenman is at his strongest as a defender of the autonomy of the architectural profession and its objects. To that extent I regret Derrida's influence on his work, and his is not the only such case. For much the same reason, I think Eisenman's notion of architecture as a "text" (160, 164)—based as it is on the Derridean assault on identity—is a bad idea. For objects are nothing if not a surplus never integrated into any text, into any set of relations.

But even if "self-presence" is among Derrida's least

convincing major concepts, this does not necessarily spoil Eisenman's emphasis on the "self-referentiality" of the architectural object. This is a different concept, and will therefore succeed or fail on different grounds. We have seen that Eisenman accuses both classical and post-Enlightenment architecture, up to and including functionalism, of directing architecture outside itself and into the human realm to find meaning. The most recent version of functionalist humanism is not found in modernism, he claims, but rather in the scattered tendencies that have opposed it: "In the end modernism made it possible for objects to be released from their role of 'speaking for man' to be able to 'speak for themselves,' of their own objecthood" (110). Self-referentiality is the key to modernity (113), marking as it does the end of classical mimesis or imitation (108). Eisenman sees this as a considerable improvement over the previous period, in which "there was no intrinsic value in objects."[35] As OOOish as this may sound, we must insist on the difference: for Eisenman as for the early Fried, to focus on the "object" means to exclude the human as a toxic threat, a special volatile agent able to corrode objects like nothing else. Yet the OOO view, in consonance with Latour, Scheler, and the later Fried, is that the hybrid mixture of human with nonhuman is just as much an object as anything else and leads to no special sort of ontological danger. We agree with Eisenman about the inwardness of the object but do not agree that humans need to be banished from that interior, at least not in the form of ingredients. There is no architecture without humans any more than there is art without humans, as seen earlier in the cases of Trevatt and Malinowska.

Be that as it may, Eisenman claims a powerful ally for self-referential architecture in no less a figure than Le Corbusier, whom Eisenman reads not as a functionalist "humanist" but as a full-blown "modernist" in his altered sense of the term. He argues for this in a detailed reading of the columns and stairway in Corb's Maison Dom-Ino;

filled with self-referential signs, this house breaks with the previously outward-looking tradition of humanist architecture (120). The self-referentiality of the house, Eisenman declares, establishes the difference between merely building a dwelling and actively making architecture. The importance of inscribing architectural signs within architecture is that "signification and function, unlike objecthood, can be manipulated. Objecthood, on the other hand, the properties of an entity's physical presence, is irreducible" (215). Although Eisenman uses "objecthood" as a positive term for self-reflexivity and Fried uses it as a negative one for literalism, there is an important overlap in their respective outlooks.[36] Namely, Eisenman's search for immanent signs of architecture in Maison Dom-Ino is deeply reminiscent of Fried's interpretation of Anthony Caro's tabletop sculptures.[37] When Caro approached the problem of making small sculptures that would fit on the surface of a table, he resisted the easy idea of simply producing miniature-scale versions of his previous works; after all, that would be a mere technical adjustment, leaving no internal trace in the sculptures themselves. He finally hit upon the brilliant solution of including in each tabletop piece an element that extended below the level of the table, so that the sculpture could not possibly sit on flat ground. One has to imagine that Eisenman would greatly admire what Caro did here, since it corresponds so closely to Le Corbusier's equally crafty maneuvers in Maison Dom-Ino.

But if Eisenman is to be considered a formalist rather than a functionalist, as everyone does consider him, we still need to ask more directly what he tells us about form. We have just noted his view that the proper conception of form entails that an object be cut off from primary reference to human utility. For Derridean reasons it cannot be "autonomous," but it must still be self-reflexive. This means that it must be filled with signs referring to architecture itself: it is not at all "useful" that the columns in Maison Dom-Ino are closer to the back wall than to the side walls, but this is still an interesting sign enabling us to conceive of the building as being possibly extended away from the front wall without being widened. Earlier we encountered Eisenman's view that form is not primarily visual, insofar as a building must be experienced over a certain period of time (8). The consequent need to hold it together in memory entails further that it should refer to some archetypal solid, at least for the young Eisenman (9). Beyond this, it is worth noting that for Eisenman as for so many modernists, a building's façade is supposedly of less interest than the plan and the section (112). Perhaps his major objection here to the postmodernist historicisms of Graves and Venturi is the way they treat the façade as a kind of painted surface, which fails to get at the heart of what architecture is about, though Eisenman is surely even more bothered by the semantic dimension of Graves's historicist turn.[38] Graves abandoned "the rich sectional manipulation of his early work" and "seems now more intent on a deductive mannerism—leaving his volumes drained of their former energy and relying instead on 'historical puns' which cannot be made in space but rather on the surface" (109). In short, "sectional and volumetric energy does not transform easily into historical allusion" (109). By turning our backs on Graves, we can have a self-referential architectural object, loaded with signs of itself and focused more on space than on surface—though I have argued that the obstructions of function in Houses III and VI run at cross-purposes to this model by denying to the internal spaces of these houses their usual role as background medium. Perhaps more interesting is Eisenman's plan to replace the dialectic of form and function with a new one internal to form itself. The original "thesis" of this new dialectic is the classical method of "transforming some pre-existent geometric or Platonic solid" (87) while leaving traces of the original, simple form. Averse to the humanist roots of this method, Eisenman introduces its dialectical "antithesis," in which architecture results instead from the simplification of a more complex initial situation of a "pre-existent set of non-specific spatial entities" (87). The "synthesis" of these tendencies—distortion of the simple, condensation of the complex—is what Eisenman has in mind when he speaks of modernism in his personal sense of the term.

One of the initially puzzling features of Eisenman's career, at least if viewed from the standpoint of art criticism, is his joint association with both formalism and conceptualism. After all, in the high modernist criticism of Greenberg and Fried, the formal and the conceptual are rigorously separated, which explains their shared contempt for Duchamp and later conceptual art. While it is true that neither of these critics much likes the word "formalism," in its Kantian sense it applies very well to both of them, given their near-total exclusion of factors stemming from outside the work itself. But true to their Kantian tendencies, they have even less use for "conceptualism," which is rigorously excluded by the principles of the *Critique of Judgment.* To view an artwork as the outcome or topic of a concept is to treat art as a paraphrasable literal experience rather than an aesthetic one; it is to repeat the error of Husserl in making conceptuality something different in kind from other forms of human comportment, while missing that objects themselves differ from all such comportment. For Eisenman, by contrast, the formal and the conceptual seem to be one and the same. We have seen how he reads Maison Dom-Ino in formal terms, and what that means is that the house is riddled with signs of its own objecthood. Eisenman also speaks favorably of the minimalists in a way that Fried does not.[39] In the architect's words: "The work of such people as Robert Morris and Donald Judd seems to have a similar purpose: to take meaning away from objects in the sense of meaning which is received from an aesthetic experience, or the meaning which is received from a representational image. Here objects have no meaning other than as the object itself" (13). From the minimalist case, as from that of Maison Dom-Ino, we find that "a conceptual structure is that aspect of the visible form . . . which is intentionally put in the form to provide access to the inner form or universal formal relationships." In this respect, "the fundamental difference between art and architecture is that the idea of architecture demands the idea of an object presence, while the idea of art does not" (15). This is debatable, insofar as sculpture also demands an object presence, but since Eisenman has excluded both function and semantic context from the picture, he has limited options for differentiating architecture from minimalist sculpture.

The option he seems to prefer is to say that architecture has the potential not only to design buildings in accordance with a concept but also to design buildings that are themselves concepts. We have already mentioned the conceptual aspects of Maison Dom-Ino, although Caro's tabletop sculptures call into question whether only architecture can make conceptual objects in this sense. What is interesting to note is that Duchamp's urinal clearly fails the conceptual litmus test for Eisenman, since it gains its "conceptual" side only from the gallery context in which it is shockingly placed, not from anything inscribed conceptually in the urinal itself. Although in educated circles one is repeatedly expected to marvel at Duchamp's radical gesture, in an Eisenmanian sense the urinal turns out to be nothing more than a tired "humanist" device. There can be no Duchamp effect in built architecture, both because architecture produces its own context and because it will always contain "the ideas of functionally and semantically weighted objects such as walls, bathrooms, doors, closets, ceilings" (16). This entails that "lines which are columns, planes which are walls, must always because of the fact of gravity, hold something up. . . . The ground plane will always be semantically different from the roof plane, and the entry plane acknowledges the difference from exterior to interior" (16). But Eisenman holds that these need to have their functions suppressed in favor of "some primary reading as a notation in a conceptual context" (17), like the rear columns of Maison Dom-Ino or the lower extension of a Caro tabletop sculpture. The real trick is "finding the means of expressing the conceptual aspect so that it is in some way apparent to the viewer" (17).

Eisenman wants to avoid the "semantic" way of doing this, as when "Le Corbusier essentially took the forms of known objects—from machines, ships, and aircraft . . . [so as] to force a shift in meaning through [their] appearance in a new context" (20). In this respect there is a trace of Duchamp in Le Corbusier to go with his regular shot of Picasso. Eisenman prefers the method of the disturbingly brilliant fascist architect Giuseppe Terragni, whose buildings are not free of semantic reference to known Renaissance forms, but "divest such type forms of their traditional meaning, and instead use the formal type as a deep-level syntactic referent to which his specific forms correspond" (20). The idea of "deep syntax" may be surprising, since what we normally expect to find in the depths is *meaning*: semantics, not syntax. Or at least that is the approach of Noam Chomsky in *Cartesian Linguistics,* a book that heavily influenced the Eisenman of the 1960s. It is also the approach of the philosopher Husserl, who treats the "deep" level of intentional objects as a conceptually graspable essence, knowable to the mind but never to the senses. But architect that he is, Eisenman is aware that there is no possibility of dispensing with the sensual to get straight to the conceptual, despite his low regard for phenomenology (18). This is why he has no wish to set up any sort of semantic "code" for architecture in which every element would have a directly conceptual meaning. Instead, he seeks a deep level of "formal universals which are inherent in any form or formal construct" (23). Without elaboration he mentions the possibility of "spatial sequences," but there was already a more concrete example in Eisenman's earliest work, when he discussed the way that primary solids all break down into forms that are either "linear" (oblong, cone) or "centroidal" (square block, sphere), combinable in different ways (corkscrew) to yield certain joint effects (3–9). The real trick, he tells us once more, is to find some method by which "the universals of the [deep] conceptual structure are transformed by some device to a surface structure and thus capable of receiving meaning" (24).

This proclaimed need for a conceptual architecture is closely connected with the issue of time. We have seen that the early Eisenman rejected the visual conception of form, in large part because architecture is more kinetic than visual; the experience of a building is woven from a series of memories, and memory is less taxed if it is anchored to relatively simple forms, as "Gestalt psychologists have conclusively demonstrated" (9). But this full experience "is conceptual [and so] must have clarity of concept; and therefore its argument must be intellectually as well as visually comprehensible" (9). What does time add to our notion of conceptual architecture? In his somewhat exasperated 1990 open letter to a typically finicky Derrida, Eisenman argues that architecture is not just a two-term relation between the surface play of signs and the purported depth—rejected by Derrida—of Heideggerian Being. This dialectic of presence and absence misses architecture's crucial third term, "presentness," which Eisenman claims to use in a sense different from Fried's. What Eisenman intends in referring to presentness is that the form/function bond must be loosened, since "the presentness of architecture is irreducible to the presence of its signs."[40] He draws on Rosalind Krauss to assert that Fried gets it wrong by remaining trapped in the "metaphysics of presence," but this seems to be another moment where he follows Derrida too closely.[41] We recall that Fried found it too theatrical when Tony Smith drove down the unfinished New Jersey turnpike rather than having a direct and immediate experience of a visual artwork. For Krauss this means that Fried is calling for an immediate unity of the art object in an instant, and for Derrideans any talk of a single instant is already the metaphysics of presence; time slips and slides and is never conceivable as a "now."[42] But this is the same conflation of "present" as a temporal instant and "present" as direct accessibility that one finds among Derrideans and mainstream Heideggerians alike. In Heidegger we have a thinker who fully accepts a time made of instants—despite the widespread assumption to the contrary—yet these instants are torn by ambiguities that make them anything but directly present to the mind.[43] Stated differently, the critique of the metaphysics of presence has no direct connection with the idea of processual rather than instantaneous time; time as process is something thematized by Bergson and Deleuze, not Heidegger and Derrida, despite the latter's claim to do so as well.[44]

Architecture is one of those practical activities that also works under an aesthetic imperative. We should not shy away from using a perfectly good, old-fashioned word for this imperative: *beauty*, a term one hears almost as rarely in architecture these days as in the arts. Although the usual opposite of beauty is thought to be ugliness, both are aesthetic phenomena that differ only in attracting or repelling us, respectively. The true opposite of the beautiful—as well as the ugly—is the literal, and I have contended that the literal occurs whenever an object seems to be nothing more than a "bundle of qualities." The vast majority of buildings are not actively ugly but blandly literal. If pure functionalism were followed, it would generate nothing but literal edifices indistinguishable from their sum total of visual and practical qualities; thus we can see that most of the architects called functionalists are already something more, since one could never achieve a reputation on the basis of mere literalism. For this reason the term "functionalist" is best understood not as referring to sheer literalism in building, which occurs seldom enough among substantial figures, but as a polemical objection to arbitrary ornament, or to form that has no basis other than external reference to history. In any case, the antidote to literalism is always to create a split between the object itself and its qualities, loosening the bond between them, a split performed by humans but enabled more readily by some objects than others. Such a rift announces that we are in the presence of something either beautiful or ugly rather than literal. This is aesthetic experience. Insofar as the qualities of aesthetic experience always exist in relation to a beholder, this means that aesthetic experience can also be interpreted as a split between the thing itself and its relations with beholders and other things, something Derrida and Eisenman cannot countenance due to their outright rejection of self-identical objects.

We recall that Kant excludes function from the realm of pure beauty due to its outward reference, which strips it of any autonomy; as a result, he assigns architecture a relatively low status among the arts. In this connection, we saw that Sullivan's motto "form follows function" can be read as a kind of bargaining with Kant, the most powerful aesthetic voice of recent centuries: "Yes, I admit that this object functions. But at least its form relates only to its function, not to stupid historical relics like caryatid columns or gargoyles or Renaissance porticoes." Alongside this functionalization of form, which tends to overweight the visible side of form, we might propose a formalization of function, to be discussed in the next section. As for Le Corbusier, his functionalist-sounding praise of bridges and engineers has a mainly polemical use against decadent historicism. His real concern, quite openly expressed, is with *beauty* and *art*. His recommendation for achieving them is through an intriguing combination of simple parts, so that form is again a matter of the surface—much as it was for Picasso in his cubist period—although not in relation to function, despite his widespread functionalist reputation. Eisenman's position is openly formalist, whether in the "medium Eisenman" sense that he treats function as a mere causal precondition of architecture that need not be emphasized or the "spicy Eisenman" sense of his deliberately subverting function. We also saw that he would like to replace the form/function dialectic with one between two possibilities of form: distortion of the simple and condensation of the complex. Much like Fried, Eisenman wants to sever the object's link with the human being; unlike Fried, he has no come-to-Manet moment when he realizes that such severance is impossible, that the human will always be an ingredient of aesthetics even when the work exceeds the grasp of the human beholder. It feels as if Eisenman is tacitly responding to Kant that architecture is not really functional, and that it therefore deserves aesthetic acceptance. But none of the three positions we have covered—Sullivan's functionalism, Eisenman's formalism, or Le Corbusier's intermediate position—challenges Kant in the heartland of his aesthetic philosophy by arguing that function, too, has its autonomy. The more direct rebuke to Kant would be to show that architectural function is formalizable, that it can be zeroed, without transforming this zeroed function into another deep form of the sort we might just as well find in sculpture.

Autonomous Function

Kant's *Critique of Pure Reason*, the central masterpiece of modern philosophy, begins with an apparently dry exercise of cross-pollination that nonetheless generates his entire system of thought. Kant asks us to consider two pairs of opposite concepts: analytic versus synthetic and a priori versus a posteriori. An analytic judgment is one that states nothing more than a logical tautology: "Bachelors are unmarried men," or perhaps "A rose is a rose." No new content is provided by an analytic judgment. By contrast, a synthetic judgment does provide new information, whether true or false: "Greeks are less prone to suicide than other Europeans" and "Abraham Lincoln was born in 1809" (both true), or "Ducks come in twenty-nine colors" and "Lions gain the ability to fly during the full moon" (both false). There is nothing about the mere concept of Greeks that entails a low suicide rate, and nothing about Lincoln that necessitates birth in 1809 rather than some other year, let alone anything in the concept of ducks that requires that they exist in some definite number of colors. The distinction between a priori and a posteriori might seem at first to be of the very same type. An a priori judgment is one that can be made independent of all experience, which seems like a natural match for logical tautologies about bachelors and roses. A posteriori judgments are those that can be made only on the basis of experience, and this seems to fit with our statements about Greeks, Lincoln, ducks, and lions. But what interests Kant is the possibility of a mixed statement that would be both a priori and synthetic: otherwise, no cognitive certainty would be possible except in the case of empty tautologies. Kant is convinced that such statements obviously exist in the case of mathematics—in disagreement with Hume, who views mathematical statements as merely tautologies—and also holds that the foundational statements of natural science are a priori synthetic judgments. This is the lever for his famous "Copernican Revolution" in philosophy. A priori synthetic judgments are possible insofar as they are not about the world itself but about the conditions of human experience of the world. This includes our pure intuitions of space and time and the twelve categories of understanding, featuring such basic aspects of reality as the law of cause and effect.

We are now in a situation analogous to Kant's predicament, except that our differing oppositional pairs are form versus function and relational versus nonrelational. Although form is often interpreted in the sense of the visual look of a building, I have argued for form in a deeper sense than the visual sort, and form in this sense is inherently nonrelational. By contrast, function appears to be relational by necessity, since it relates to something else in the world in order to get something done. By analogy with Kant's question "How are a priori synthetic judgments possible?" what we are asking here is essentially "How is nonrelational function possible?" As a reminder, there are two reasons to ask such a question: (1) If the functional side of architecture is disowned rather than maintained, we have only a weak basis for distinguishing architecture from sculpture. (2) If function is not autonomized or zeroed, then it cannot enter the aesthetic realm, and will be nothing but a programmatic coat hanger over which arbitrary aesthetic forms are draped. We can also restate our question as "How is nonliteral relation possible?" This has nothing to do with Derrida's insistence that there is no such thing as the literal insofar as nothing can be made present apart from the endless play of signifiers. For OOO literalism is not impossible but ubiquitous, and must be met with active countermeasures. Literalism means that an object is misidentified with a bundle of qualities, whether known or unknown, thereby neglecting the powerful looseness of their relation.

Kant not only defined but also successfully pursued his question of how a priori synthetic judgments are possible; the result was his entire philosophy, more sweeping in its influence than any since ancient Greece. But as for the question of how nonliteral relation is possible, Kant never posed it; in fact, his aesthetic theory actively forbids it. The experience of beauty is for him the textbook example of an experience both nonliteral and nonrelational. Beauty cannot be defined by its agreeable relation to me; it cannot be paraphrased in terms of a concept or other literal meaning; it is not the mere product of foolproof rules, since no rules can be given for producing it.[45] Yet the beautiful eludes necessary relationship with any specific characteristics, and in this respect it is exactly what we seek: the object in loose relationship with its own qualities. For the Kantian tradition of aesthetics, the most horrific relation, which must be avoided at any price, is that between the art object and the human beholder, for this relation is the very font of literalism. We saw that in Kant's case the beholder's faculty of judgment, shared by all humans, is the source of beauty; the art object itself is in some sense dispensable. We saw further that the formalism of Greenberg and the early Fried—like that of Eisenman in architecture—reverses this emphasis, excluding the beholder so that the object is left to shine alone. What both solutions overlook is that no aesthetic experience can occur if we have merely an object or a beholder in isolation. This entails that object and beholder need each other, and thus we seem to be thrown back on literalism. Yet we have already seen how this is avoided in the case of metaphor. The beholder steps in for the absent object and forms a union with its qualities. This relation is loose by definition, since there is no sense in which the reader of a poem really begins to smell like a rose or darken like the wine-dark sea.

The metaphor is a new object, one produced from a union between the beholder and the qualities the absent object left behind. Yet precisely because this confederation is so difficult and implausible—otherwise, the result would be literal statement—the two terms remain distinct. This very duality explains how nonliteral relation is possible, since the way aesthetic experience zeroes or deliteralizes relation now becomes clear. In the case of Homer's "wine-dark sea" it takes a relation between objects—between me and the dark sea—and turns it into a relation on the interior of a larger object. I am still myself, but am performing an absent sea by means of wine-dark qualities: and all of this on the inside of the new object produced by the successful metaphor. Stated differently, we have taken a previously external relation between two separate terms and substantialized that relation by placing it on the inside of a new object. Strange though this terminology may sound, the notion that objects have interiors is as old as Leibniz.

To describe this process as "substantialization" will no doubt meet with resistance. After all, for a century and more we have been trained to debunk all forms of "reification," "hypostatization," and "fetishization" as costly intellectual blunders. But there is an important new element here. All of these critical terms refer to situations in which something that is not truly an object is treated as an object. But the present case is the opposite: we are taking something that is not initially a unified object—myself plus the sea— and actually turning it into one. Fetish becomes reality by definition. The aesthetic object undeniably exists, since each of us has experienced it on many occasions. Just as undeniably, it is different from anything that happens when the sea and I are merely placed in contiguity. The sea and I are not just two independent beings, but more like hydrogen and oxygen in a molecule of water. Yet the metaphor itself—like the molecule—remains autonomous, fending off meddling external influence. Architecturally speaking, consider the way in which a concrete box plus a door is more than the two elements considered separately, or the manner in which a thousand bricks stacked into an arch is not the same thing as those bricks sitting stacked in a warehouse.[46] In these ways, a relation can be de-relationized or deliteralized. This is the way to zero artistic form, but we still have no idea how to zero, aestheticize, or substantialize function itself without turning a building into mere sculpture. We have said that there are two things that make architecture different from visual art, one of them function and the other time. Since the latter turns out to be somewhat easier to deal with, let's begin with time.

There are many distinctions to be drawn with respect to time, such as that between spatialized cinematic time and flowing real time (Bergson) or the one between clock time and lived existential time (Heidegger). My concern here is not with these, but with what might be called the difference between clock time and calendar time. In a sense everything belongs to calendar time, because everything is historical and shifts in meaning in terms of both (a) how tradition develops around it and (b) how a work strikes us differently at different stages of life or of history. This is Rossi's topic when he speaks of monumentality, and works of visual art are just as capable of monumental status as landmark works of architecture. Clock time is where we find the real difference between visual art and architecture, since whatever surfeit of detail a painter like Hieronymus Bosch might provide, his paintings still have instantaneous "presentness" in a way that cannot be true of a building. We experience time in a specious present, and this is where a painting can and does appear. When it comes to a building, however, the work of memory is needed to tie together all the experiences of a first stroll around the outside and the inside alike. Our later experiences of it become increasingly of a monumental sort, laden as they are with sediments of personal and historical experience accrued since the initial experience.

These temporal encounters require not just legibility but a certain degree of richness as well. Consider the difference between two major buildings by Gehry. His 1997 Guggenheim

Frank Gehry, Museo Guggenheim Bilbao, Spain. Creative Commons Attribution-Share Alike 2.0 Generic. Photograph by Sergio S.C.

Museum in Bilbao is one of the most celebrated works of recent architecture, ranked number twelve in its century by the poll in Mayne's book.[47] Bilbao is a relatively small city that had suffered from economic hardship and civil strife, but is now on tourism "bucket lists" largely thanks to this building. It has already achieved Rossian monumental status; whatever happens in Bilbao over the next century or two will shape the building further and be shaped by it in turn. Yes, in calendar time it is a monument. But in terms of clock time, its internal complexity falls short of that on the exterior. It is certainly a pleasure to walk in a circuit around the Guggenheim, enjoying ever-shifting views while encountering famous artworks such as a Jeff Koons flower puppy and a Louise Bourgeois giant spider. But there is a reason that most photographs of this building show it from the outside. The interior space is not unattractive, and even has a tangible Gehry signature in places. But it is too quickly explored, lacking in complexity, and few visitors stay for very long; all the fun to be had is on the exterior. In other words, it is all a bit too sculpture-like. But how different the experience is at a more recent Gehry monument: the 2014 Fondation Louis Vuitton building in Paris. Here the flower- or sail-like structure is already highly attractive, and I happen to prefer it to the monotonous metallic surfaces of Bilbao. But the interior is what makes all the difference, especially the surprising roof terrace, reached by a nondescript stairway entrance. The clock time of the Louis Vuitton building is rich, and I found myself not wanting to leave. Its relative isolation does tend to make it more like an artwork than an urban monument à la Bilbao, though the always potent calendar time of Paris may take care of that issue eventually.

We saw that aesthetic form is zeroed by substantialization of the relation between beholder and work, bringing this relation onto the interior of a new object. A similar process occurs when it comes to the zeroing of time. Any given moment of experience is an object only in the weak sense that, in retrospect, I can make it the object of my reflections. An easier way to zero time is to string together a series of experiences, with our memory pushing them together like heterogeneous masses. This can also be done in a diary or memoir, not to mention a novel by Proust. But architecture has the special method of anchoring these experiences in a solid physical object, lending the support of granite or marble to the innately feebler webs of human recollection. One implication is that architecture is less in need of "withdrawal" than are instantaneous arts such as painting, since here the role of direct presence is less threatening. Any given view of even the most transparent architectural form is destined to be no more than a tiny facet of an inherently temporal experience. This does not mean that architecture is compelled to make use of a rich succession of variable experiences, that it can never aim at more minimal effects. But it does imply that temporal complexity is a valuable resource for the discipline, one that should be suppressed not from mere forgetfulness but only so as to accentuate achievements along a different front. I have often been critical of Merleau-Ponty's view that "the house itself is not the house seen from nowhere, but the house seen from everywhere," including earlier in this book.[48] And I insist that this remains a false ontological account of the reality of the house, which cannot be produced from a sum of views. Nonetheless, the temporal experience of architecture is in fact "the house seen from everywhere," though substantialized or zeroed into an object that is something different from the house itself. It seems to give us the impossible: a God's-eye view of the total being of the building.

The aestheticization of function is a different sort of problem. We have seen that we cannot do this in Eisenman's manner of suppressing function or subverting it outright, since we are then dangerously close to sculpture, and some of the most precious differentiating resources of architecture are lost. Now as ever, the way to zero function is to substantialize it. Yet the problem here is the opposite of the case of visual art. There, we began with an ostensible difference between beholder and work, which we countered by unifying them in a single object. In the case of function, however, the initial situation is one in which the terms are already unified. As Heidegger famously shows, function entails a unified total effect, one that is generally disrupted only when something goes wrong. As a rule we do not think of floorboards, windows, doorways, and HVAC infrastructure as separate physical beings, but only as a total effect. Therefore, the way to substantialize this function is not— as in visual art—through the fusion of independent terms into a single entity, since this is a *fait accompli*. Rather, the opposite gesture is needed: the various terms of the function must become slightly detached from each other, though only as much as can be done without halting the function. This means, among other things, that columns through the living space will usually not do. In visual art, as in metaphor, we deliteralize through theatrically performing the unification of ourselves and the work. In architecture—though it may also make use of explicit metaphor—we deliteralize function by cracking its elements slightly free from their mutual relations. As seen, this might entail a slight decomposition of purpose, pushing as close to failure as possible. Alternatively, it might entail that the function be rendered less specific, and thereby withheld slightly from any relation in particular. Rossi has already shown that this is what monuments do, and in a sense, all the possible methods of zeroing are ways of monumentalizing objects.

After Deconstructivism

Needless to say, the Deconstructivist trend does not exhaust the sum total of significant architecture in the past half century: one should also mention Mayne, Renzo Piano, and numerous others of their generation not included in the famous 1988 MoMA show. Even so, that exhibition was surely the one canonical moment since the breakdown of high modernism that brought together a large number of figures of undoubted significance for the discipline. Since we have seen that Deconstructivism included or prefigured aspects of Heidegger and Deleuze along with the main Derridean current, the MoMA show can also be regarded as the central event for the dialogue between philosophy and architecture. We recall Wigley's statement from the close of his catalog essay: "The episode [of the Deconstructivism show] will be short-lived. The architects will proceed in different directions. . . . This is not a new style."[49] Even if not a new style, it might have been something of even greater long-term interest: an ur-style capable of supporting multiple variants, and hence capable of further development in different directions.

In a 1993 article, Kipnis tries to make sense of what has happened since the MoMA show by speaking of two rival tendencies: "De-Formation," which "emphasizes the role of new aesthetic forms and therefore the visual in the engenderment of new spaces," and "InFormation," which "deemphasizes the role of aesthetic form in favor of new institutional form, and therefore of programs and events."[50] He lists Eisenman and Gehry as exemplars of the first group, and Koolhaas and Tschumi of the second. He thus omits three figures from the MoMA show: Coop Himmelb(l)au, Hadid, and Libeskind. Of these three, Hadid could most easily be linked with the discourse of continuity. Her MoMA project, an elite club in Hong Kong, certainly qualifies as Deconstructivist in tone: "The most radical decentering occurs when the upper pair of beams is pulled apart, vertically, enough from the lower pair to construct a deep void which is completely isolated from traditional assumptions about building. The usual hierarchies and orthogonal order are missing."[51] But of course she is now better known as the "Queen of the Curve" for the gracefully flowing lines of her buildings.[52]

Zaha Hadid, Library and Learning Center, WU Wien. Creative Commons Attribution-Share Alike 3.0 Austria. Photograph by Böhringer Friedrich.

And while it is doubtful that Hadid was ever very interested in Deleuze, Schumacher's effort to theorize the work of her firm is saturated with Deleuzian ideas of continuity, even if Luhmann is the most explicit referent.[53] The Kipnis of 1993 was heavily involved in appropriating the Deleuzian legacy, instead, for the circle of the now post–Derridean Eisenman, even if this was more concretely the work of Lynn. Yet the latter's assessment that Gehry's Santa Monica house is all about continuity is at least somewhat counterintuitive. And the "Deleuzian" shift of Eisenman, as in his master plan for Rebstockpark in Frankfurt, is still too rectilinear to qualify as such, despite the references to folding and the homage to Deleuze's ingenious misreading of Leibniz as a philosopher of the continuous.[54] But while it would be strange to speak of Hadid's post-1988 career as displaying a "Deconstructivist" aesthetic, the word is eminently apt with respect to Libeskind, despite the partial continuist flirtation of his Imperial War Museum North in Manchester. Libeskind has generally stuck with his trademark vocabulary of disruption and dislocation, and his recent work might be the showcase of any hypothetical Deconstructivism exhibition held today. The same goes for the post-rooftop work of Coop Himmelb(l)au, which continues to make extensive use of the twisted but linear forms highlighted in Wigley's catalog essay (as in the Seat of the European Central Bank, Frankfurt, 2015).

We return to Kipnis's "Toward a New Architecture," first published in 1993, the landmark year of his circle's shift from Derrida to Deleuze. What everyone has been fleeing, Kipnis notes, is postmodern collage. Like any other style, "[as] it becomes the prevailing institutional practice, it loses both its contradictory force and its affirmative incoherence. Rather than destabilizing an existing context, it operates more and more to inscribe its own institutional space."[55] Where can architectural aesthetics go after collage? It is the view of Kipnis that the InFormation camp (Koolhaas and Tschumi) thinks there is nowhere it can possibly go. This movement "posits that the exhaustion of collage is tantamount to rendering irrelevant all aesthetic gestures," leaving no role for further advances in style.[56] Hence the default program-heavy style of the InFormationists, a stripped-down modernism of orthogonal forms, "often stressing the blankness by using the forms as screens for projected images."[57] As a favored example, Kipnis cites Tschumi's Le Fresnoy arts center, opened in 1997 in Tourcoing, France, near the Belgian border. The initial site offered built-in incentives toward some sort of historical postmodernism. As Tschumi's website informs us: "The site holds buildings from a 1920s leisure complex that included cinema, ballroom dancing, skating, and horseback riding. Although the existing structures could have been demolished to make way for new construction, they contained extraordinary spaces whose large dimensions exceeded what the limited project budget could supply."[58] With demolition ruled out, the obvious solution might have been a collage approach. Instead, as Kipnis reports, "Tschumi . . . enveloped the entire complex within a partially enclosed modern roof to create a cohesive graft," with the result being "a blank, monolithic unity whose incongruity is internalized."[59] If the "spicy" Eisenman tends to turn everything into façade, Tschumi attempts the opposite feat. While this does offer unique programmatic possibilities, Kipnis reads it more as a matter of producing a novel space, "with a system of catwalks and stairs, visually interlacing them with cuts, partial enclosures, ribbon windows, and broad transparencies."[60]

For evidence of a purer commitment to program among the InFormationists, Kipnis naturally turns to Koolhaas. In a 1996 article on his then-recent work, Kipnis proposes that whereas Eisenman demands an end to "humanist" architecture due to developments in (Derridean) philosophy, Koolhaas sees it as ending due to the elevator.[61] This witticism conceals a false choice, since Derrida and the elevator both provide new possible outlooks on architectural reality. It is certainly true that the well-read Eisenman has long been the thinking person's architect, and that by contrast, "Koolhaas has been the most single-minded [of the 1988 Deconstructivists] in deriving his trajectory and techniques from a frank meditation on architecture rather than from contemporary philosophy or cultural theory."[62] The intention is evidently to link Koolhaas with not just programmatic but also *technical* innovations, and thus to set up a classic opposition between formalism and functionalism—or rather, "programmatism." One must admit that such a reading has some evidence in its favor. Kipnis notes Koolhaas's "rejection of the

renewed call for the supremacy of beauty in architecture,"
after an early dig at his tendency toward "cheap, even ugly,
construction."[63] On a positive note, Kipnis observes that "a
curious feature of Koolhaas's career is the unusual number of [failed] competition entries it has produced that have
come to assume the status of paradigmatic projects, even
contemporary masterworks."[64] Among the most famous is
his entry for the Tate Modern in London, eventually built
instead by Herzog & de Meuron. The reaction of Kipnis to
Koolhaas's famous design is a unique mixture of awe and
barely restrained disgust:

> On the one hand, the OMA [Office for Metropolitan Archi-
> tecture] entry to the Tate/Bankside competition is the most
> aggressive, most meticulously disestablishing design ever
> to emerge from the practice. On the other hand, as a work
> of architecture it is disappointing, even desperate. It must
> be said that the design might well have led to a sensational
> situation for experiencing art, but if it had, it would have
> been an achievement that hurried the extinction not only of
> the museum but of the discipline of architecture.[65]

How so, exactly? As Kipnis summarizes the project, "Form
is suppressed, program is augmented, nonspecific flows and
events are encouraged, vestigial spaces are deployed, and
poché is erased." Restated briefly: "Koolhaas dissolves the
Tate/Bankside into pure organization."[66] This threatens the
ruin of architecture because "it is a work of urban infrastructure . . . whose fundamental measure is not aesthetic
quality but performance over time at maximum use."[67] From
a OOO standpoint this sounds perfectly dismal: a cynical
degeneration of architecture into programmatic literalism,
even if a nonspecific infrastructural one. But we still need
to decide if this is the best possible interpretation of what
Koolhaas is up to.

One alternative comes from a widespread countertradi-
tion in the discipline, which interprets Koolhaas as a formalist in disguise: as someone who uses programmatic sales

pitches mainly to seduce clients into accepting his unusual new forms.[68] An example is the Beijing CCTV tower, completed in 2012, which many in the Chinese public jokingly liken to a pair of men's trousers. The architect's own programmatic explanation is that the design links the successive stages of television production in a single line: one that first ascends vertically and then shifts into two nearly perpendicular lateral legs before descending another vertical line to the ground. It is easy enough to find architects who regard this as a pretext for what is basically meant as a novel tower form. Mark Alan Hewitt expresses this view in a bluntly polemical assessment, denouncing the "slippery" Koolhaas as one of a group of architects "obsessed with creating dazzling 'new' forms for large buildings" and guilty of "failing to justify their increasingly formalistic play with sculptural masses and structural pyrotechnics." Delivering nothing but "formal one-liners," such designers indulge in the "inane, self-contradictory conceit . . . that today's designers employ to conceal the fashion branding that links [them to] the latest Prada sportswear collection." He also accuses such architects of "justify[ing] their empty formal experiments in terms that engineers would find hard to believe, using pseudo-functionalist rhetoric."[69]

We now seem far indeed from Kipnis's apparently straightforward reading of Koolhaas as an antiformalist. Yet even in Kipnis there are traces of a possible formalist Koolhaas. For instance, he observes that Koolhaas's work "offers little resistance . . . to the intoxications of consumer culture."[70] While this would sound like a brutal slam coming from any critical theorist, from a formalist sympathizer like Kipnis it is almost a sign of recognition: Hey, this guy may be one of us! After all, his point is surely not that the "De-Formationists" Eisenman and Gehry are active resisters of consumerism—a Gehry-inspired Kentucky Fried Chicken restaurant recently survived a Los Angeles fire. It is true that he later tries to grant Koolhaas a political intention: "[His]

Rem Koolhaas, model of CCTV Headquarters, Beijing. Creative Commons Attribution-Share Alike 3.0 Unported, 2.5 Generic, 2.0 Generic, and 1.0 Generic licenses. Photograph by Pvt pauline.

work never resists authority; it sabotages authority from within."[71] But since Kipnis is widely known as a "politically incorrect" figure disinclined to flatter the self-righteous, I take this sentence to refer not to some covert leftist stratagem by OMA but to Kipnis's view that Koolhaas is an antiformalist architect of human freedom.[72] More important is Kipnis's obvious admiration for the unbuilt Koolhaas opera house in Cardiff, Wales, which he describes in suitably formalist terms: "A pavilion crashes into a large box and scrolls into an aneurysm at the point of collision. Yet, the awkwardness of the massing is compelling, etching instantly into memory. No architect who has seen the scheme could ever fail to sketch it later."[73] Surely, any architectural work that is easy to sketch from memory has already passed the supreme test of form. Kipnis does go on to give a plausible programmatic analysis of the design. And furthermore, the "large, white box" element of the opera house fits his theory that the InFormationists are satisfied in formal terms with a modernism of blank monoliths whose articulations thrive only on programmatic interiors. Yet it is hard to deny that the real action in the design comes from the collision of the three separate masses, and the crash of the large box into two utterly heterogeneous elements could almost be read as a comical challenge to Kipnis's "monolith" take on the InFormationists, if Koolhaas had been aware of it when designing Cardiff.

Between these two alternatives, how might we choose? Is Koolhaas someone who has turned his back on aesthetics in the name of a maximal bureaucratic streamlining of programmatic event spaces? Or is he primarily a designer of form, in the negative sense of a shallow hunter after novel computer-generated brands? It seems to me that neither of these options gets it right. Rather than a programmatist or a formalist, Koolhaas is perhaps better interpreted as a premonition of zero-functionalism. This is what gives him his compelling novelty, which leads even Kipnis to cite the statement of a puzzled authority—who turns out to be Kipnis himself—that the head designer of OMA is "the Le Corbusier of our times."[74] It is once again Kipnis who provides the resources for a reading contrary to his own. He draws a distinction between the "garden principle" and the "infrastructural tenet," the latter referring to the creed of Koolhaas himself. Kipnis defines the garden principle as follows: "Every [criterion] of conventional architectural judgment remains dedicated to a conception of architecture as being at its best when a building is empty."[75] We already know that Koolhaas cannot be too interested in empty buildings, given his commitment to maximum possible performance; architectural performance invariably involves people. We now seem to be confronted with a familiar opposition: the garden principle is the guiding light of formalism, and the infrastructural tenet is to be paired instead with programmatism. But in something of a surprise, Kipnis places both form and program on the side of the garden principle: "The architectural concept of program is entirely complicit with the garden principle. Pre-scripting activity with efficiency and functional specificity limits use and moves people quickly to and from their destinations, reducing distraction."[76] Where does this leave Koolhaas, if his infrastructural tenet no longer has access to either form or program? In discussing OMA's Tate Modern proposal, Kipnis has already spoken of "*nonspecific* flows and events."[77] Along the same lines is his wonderfully worded claim that "radical reduction of the expectations of a given design brief is characteristic of Koolhaas's recent approach to a project. More like a sadist than a surgeon, he has begun to knife the brief, hacking away its fat, even its flesh, until he has exposed its nerve."[78] Kipnis also reads Koolhaas as an architect radically devoted to "freedom."[79] But this freedom should not be read in a political sense of liberty from oppression, even if the new left finds much to appreciate in Koolhaas; neither should we read it as an exclusively human freedom. Instead, it is freedom in the sense of "radical reduction": a deliteralization in which content is hacked away in the manner of fat and flesh. For Kipnis this implies inhumane horrors, such as the death of aesthetics and the consequent death of architecture. Yet the case of Cardiff shows Kipnis's awareness that Koolhaas takes delight in using his radical reduction to generate unexpected novelties of form. Yes, blank modernist monoliths can also be found on his curriculum vitae. But these might be reinterpreted as literalist ballast meant to call our attention, by way of contrast, to the radical reductions on the interior. It would be much like Salvador Dalí using the most traditional illusionistic portrayal of three-dimensional space as a deliberate dead weight to support so many hallucinogenic figures.[80]

On this note we return to the question of zero-form, which initially seemed easier to attain than zero-function. For now that we have seen Koolhaas attain something like zero-function through "radical reduction" and the "infrastructural tenet," we might ponder an analogous radical reduction of form, and wonder if the path of least resistance was some sort of minimalism. But this would get things backward; as discussed earlier, the problem with form is really the reverse. That is to say, the radical reduction of program works not because radical reduction itself is inherently good, but because program suffers from a congenital excess of relations. Stated differently, function is an arena surprisingly ripe for abstraction. But since the initial condition of form is a zeroed nonrelationism rather than a glut of interaction (as with function), it is necessary here to move in the opposite direction. Rather than a functional subtraction of quasi-autonomous units from an initial holistic union, the aspiring formalist faces the predicament of excessively isolated units in need of being strung together by addition. This is the sought-for complexity, which Kipnis is surely right cannot be found in collage, so often held together only by the most arbitrary willfulness. We have seen that architectural clock time, when anchored in a convincing physical unit, is one powerful way to string heterogeneous things together in a chain. The proper approach to zero-form would be to pass Koolhaas on the escalator in the opposite direction: with a mission of "radical production" rather than reduction, fusing together things that were initially distinct. If zero-function decontextualizes, zero-form is tasked primarily with producing new contexts. This is why form and function cannot be dissolved into a neutral prior medium: they work at cross-purposes, confronted with opposite initial burdens.

CONCLUDING MAXIMS

BY WAY OF CONCLUSION, LET'S SUMMARIZE THE PRINCIPLES that have emerged from this book, along with related thoughts left unstated so far. This should prove more useful to the reader than additional pages of reworded summaries.

■ *Formalism is true,* for the simple reason that the world is not a finely shaded gradient or web of relations but a set of self-contained systems whose communication must be established or earned rather than presupposed.

■ *Kantian formalism is false,* since there is no a priori reason to exclude specific types of things from aesthetic or other systems—whether beholders, observers, occupants, inhabitants, functions, societies, or politics.

■ Because Kantian formalism is false, *Kant's aesthetic suspicion of architecture is unwarranted.* There is no good reason to exclude functions from aesthetics, as long as they are de-relationized—and that means deliteralized.

- We insist on *an absolute gulf between the literal and the aesthetic,* even if context might be needed to determine whether we are dealing with one or the other. It is not that literalism is impossible for the Derridean reason that nothing ever becomes directly present. Though I agree with the point against presence, that is not what literalism is about. Rather, it hinges on the Humean claim that an object is merely a bundle of qualities. The entire point of OOO is that the object–quality relation is necessarily loose, and that such looseness can be accentuated by various aesthetic techniques.

- Buildings must serve functional and social needs, must be constructible given the current state of the art, and will often have foreseen and unforeseen political effects. But all this is *merely the precondition for architecture.* When architecture forswears aesthetics, it becomes engineering or some other discipline.

- The aesthetic side of architecture can choose to combine formal innovation with functional literalism or formal literalism with functional innovation, but it has the unique capability—foreign to visual art—of *deliteralizing both form and function,* and should not discard this advantage lightly. The term "zeroing" is another name for such deliteralization.

- The various zeroing techniques must be discovered and pursued by architects themselves. *No philosopher can pretend to legislate them,* nor does any philosopher actually attempt this.

- Since function consists of a previous unity of elements, *the zeroing of function will initially follow the path of decomposing such unity,* with Heidegger's tool-analysis as its philosophical model. This might involve existing Deconstructivist techniques, but could just as easily entail a radical stripping down or flexibilization of function.

Another way of putting it is that function can be "monu-mentalized" in the Rossian sense of detaching it from all current and possible uses.

■ Since form consists of a previous independence of for-mal elements, *the zeroing of form will initially take two steps.* First, the evident form must be zeroed into a "deep form" that resists any outward glance; second, this deep form can be strung together with others, yielding surprising combinations that generally work best if they maintain a certain memorable simplicity. The temporal aspect of architecture helps do this by conjoining dissimilar forms in sequence.

■ *There is no important philosophical difference* between archi-tectures of human experience (existing phenomenology) and those of conceptual inscription (existing formalism). Although these result in very different kinds of buildings, both miss the sense in which reality is incompletely fath-omed by experience and concepts alike.

■ An unrestrained programmatic architecture *would also have no important difference from these,* if not that such work already has a tendency to strip function down to its nervous system (Koolhaas at the Tate Modern) or to graft elements of program into unique formal conglomerations (Tschumi at Le Fresnoy).

■ A good work of architecture will tend to *break free both from its compositional elements and history on the one hand and from its social and environmental context on the other.* A building is a black box not just in the sense that it can be opened to reveal many participants but also in the sense that it is something more than those participants. This is no more "snobbish" than observing that Shakespeare's plays can travel through time and space with a distinctly invariant core, however reduced or augmented.

■ *Sociopolitical critiques of formalism in architecture bear only on its preconditions:* on the social or infrastructural duties it ought to perform. Formalism is not politically suspect, any more than poems are suspect for not attempting to save the world.

■ All work in every discipline, including but not limited to architecture, *works under a monumental imperative.* Another name for this would be a canonical imperative—that is, a work should try to be more than the product of its time and place, however difficult this may be. When approached properly, a canon is not an oppressive schoolhouse pantheon but the means for insisting that present-day work aspire to the standards of the best existing work, as well as for continually reassessing the canon itself on the basis of future breakthroughs. Where a canon is demographically exclusive, this requires that we redouble our efforts not to exclude; it does not mean that the very idea of a canon is itself politically toxic. The false alternative would be to argue that all work arising under new social or demographic conditions is inherently successful and worthy of emulation.

■ *Object-oriented approaches to architecture are not impossibly literal or professionally useless, but are already being deployed.* They are not reducible to "mystery," which already entered the field centuries ago under the headings of the picturesque and the sublime. OOO is generally too urban in spirit to be picturesque, and too focused on individual elements to be sublime. It consists of a reflection on the fourfold tensions between objects and their qualities, and is not devoted solely to the masking of inner form. Many of its techniques already exist in advance, but the same is true of the car, the computer, or any other innovation. Originality consists in new permutations of both familiar and unfamiliar elements, not in the creation of utterly unprecedented novelties out of whole cloth.

- Like visual art—but even more so, due to its explicit use of interior spaces—*architecture involves both medium and mediators,* both *studium* and *punctum.* It cannot become pure atmosphere or sheer text.

- Architects listen to philosophers not to be harangued with condescending lessons but *to dispute about areas of overlap.* Architecture requires much technical and design know-how utterly foreign to philosophy. Yet it is also an implicit statement about the nature of reality, and for this reason the architecture–philosophy dialogue is unlikely to disappear. With luck, philosophy will soon change to the point where it can learn more in return than has previously been the case. This would require a more pronounced aesthetic turn in philosophy and a shift away from the modern obsession with the onto-taxonomy of thought and world.

NOTES

Introduction

1. Harman, "Aesthetics as First Philosophy."
2. For a sample of his views, see Ruy, "Returning to (Strange) Objects."
3. Fred Scharmen, Twitter thread, April 27, 2016, https://twitter.com /sevensixfive/status/725523329654857729.
4. This is also the upshot of Bryan E. Norwood's conflicted attack in "Metaphors for Nothing," in which he responds to Todd Gannon et al., "The Object Turn."
5. Deleuze, *The Fold.*
6. See Harman, *Dante's Broken Hammer.*
7. For the thing-in-itself, see Kant's *Critique of Pure Reason.* For his ethical theory, see the *Critique of Practical Reason.* For his views on the autonomy of artworks, the *Critique of Judgment* is the place to look.
8. Hegel, *Phenomenology of Spirit.*
9. See Harman, *Art and Objects.*
10. Catherine Ingraham makes a similar point in a different context in "The Burdens of Linearity," 644.
11. Kant, *Critique of Judgment,* 77.
12. Kant, *Critique of Judgment,* 191.
13. For another treatment of these issues, see Morgan, *Kant for Architects.*
14. A fine exposition of this topic, in a more pro-Derridean spirit than my own, is Hägglund's *Radical Atheism.*

1. Architects and Their Philosophers

1. For a classic introduction to ANT, see Latour, *Reassembling the Social.*
2. For a critical but admiring treatment of Latour's philosophy, see Harman, *Prince of Networks.*
3. Hume, *A Treatise of Human Nature.*
4. Yaneva and Mommersteeg, "The Unbearable Lightness," 218.
5. Yaneva and Mommersteeg, "The Unbearable Lightness," 218–19.
6. Yaneva and Mommersteeg, "The Unbearable Lightness," 219.
7. Yaneva and Mommersteeg, "The Unbearable Lightness," 225.
8. Yaneva and Mommersteeg, "The Unbearable Lightness," 227; Whitehead, *Process and Reality.*
9. Yaneva and Mommersteeg, "The Unbearable Lightness," 227.
10. Yaneva and Mommersteeg, "The Unbearable Lightness," 225.
11. Harman, "On the Undermining of Objects"; Harman, "Undermining, Overmining, and Duomining."
12. Yaneva and Mommersteeg, "The Unbearable Lightness," 219.
13. Whitehead, *Process and Reality.*
14. See Harman, "Heidegger, McLuhan and Schumacher."
15. See, for instance, Kaufmann, *Von Ledoux bis Le Corbusier,* as well as the discussion of that book in Vidler, *Histories of the Immediate Present,* chap. 1. But note that whereas Kaufmann (and Vidler's interpretation of him) delves into the political roots of autonomy, for me autonomy is a more general philosophical notion, quite apart from the question of its historical grounding.
16. Bachelard, *The Poetics of Space.*
17. Heidegger, *Being and Time*; Harman, *Tool-Being.*
18. See Sharr, *Heidegger for Architects.*
19. Heidegger, "Building Dwelling Thinking," 347.
20. Heidegger, "Building Dwelling Thinking," 349.
21. Heidegger, "Building Dwelling Thinking," 352.
22. Heidegger, "Insight into That Which Is."
23. Harman, "Dwelling with the Fourfold."
24. Heidegger, "Building Dwelling Thinking," 357.
25. Heidegger, "Building Dwelling Thinking," 362.
26. Heidegger, "Building Dwelling Thinking," 363.
27. Pallasmaa, *The Eyes of the Skin,* 34.
28. Merleau-Ponty, *Phenomenology of Perception.*
29. Pallasmaa, *The Eyes of the Skin,* 11.
30. Pallasmaa, *The Eyes of the Skin,* 13.
31. Pallasmaa, *The Eyes of the Skin,* 63.
32. Pallasmaa, *The Eyes of the Skin,* 64.

33. Pallasmaa, *The Eyes of the Skin*, 32.
34. Norberg-Schulz, *Genius Loci*, 78–110 (Prague), 113–37 (Khartoum), 138–65 (Rome).
35. Norberg-Schulz, *Genius Loci*, 23, 24.
36. Norberg-Schulz, *Genius Loci*, 21.
37. Norberg-Schulz, *Genius Loci*, 45–46.
38. Norberg-Schulz, *Genius Loci*, 69–76.
39. Norberg-Schulz, *Genius Loci*, 182.
40. Norberg-Schulz, *Genius Loci*, 58.
41. Norberg-Schulz, *Genius Loci*, 5.
42. Norberg-Schulz, *Genius Loci*, 50.
43. Norberg-Schulz, *Genius Loci*, 65–66.
44. Zumthor, *Thinking Architecture*, 22.
45. Zumthor, *Thinking Architecture*, 24.
46. Zumthor, *Thinking Architecture*, 10, 8.
47. Zumthor, *Thinking Architecture*, 17, 18.
48. Zumthor, *Thinking Architecture*, 53, 86.
49. Zumthor, *Thinking Architecture*, 31.
50. Zumthor, *Thinking Architecture*, 86.
51. Zumthor, *Thinking Architecture*, 86–87.
52. Zumthor, *Thinking Architecture*, 77.
53. Benedikt, *Architecture beyond Experience*, viii.
54. See Buber, *I and Thou*.
55. Kant, *Critique of Judgment*, 94–95.
56. Derrida, "Point de folie." The French title is retained in the English translation.
57. Derrida and Eisenman, *Chora L Works*.
58. Johnson and Wigley, *Deconstructivist Architecture*, 10–20.
59. Johnson and Wigley, *Deconstructivist Architecture*, 7.
60. Johnson and Wigley, *Deconstructivist Architecture*, 11–12.
61. Johnson and Wigley, *Deconstructivist Architecture*, 12.
62. Johnson and Wigley, *Deconstructivist Architecture*, 12.
63. Johnson and Wigley, *Deconstructivist Architecture*, 15.
64. Johnson and Wigley, *Deconstructivist Architecture*, 15.
65. Johnson and Wigley, *Deconstructivist Architecture*, 11.
66. Shklovsky, *Theory of Prose*.
67. Aristotle, *Poetics*, 1458a, 55.
68. Johnson and Wigley, *Deconstructivist Architecture*, 17–18.
69. Johnson and Wigley, *Deconstructivist Architecture*, 18.
70. Heidegger, *Being and Time*, 233. For a Freudian rather than Heideggerian sense of the uncanny, see Vidler, *The Architectural Uncanny*.
71. Woessner, *Heidegger in America*, 254.
72. Johnson and Wigley, *Deconstructivist Architecture*, 18.

73. Johnson and Wigley, *Deconstructivist Architecture,* 16.
74. Ingraham, "Milking Deconstruction," 480.
75. Johnson and Wigley, *Deconstructivist Architecture,* 16, emphasis added.
76. Johnson and Wigley, *Deconstructivist Architecture,* 16.
77. Johnson and Wigley, *Deconstructivist Architecture,* 17.
78. Johnson and Wigley, *Deconstructivist Architecture,* 17.
79. Johnson and Wigley, *Deconstructivist Architecture,* 11.
80. Johnson and Wigley, *Deconstructivist Architecture,* 10.
81. Johnson and Wigley, *Deconstructivist Architecture,* 16.
82. Johnson and Wigley, *Deconstructivist Architecture,* 16, emphasis added.
83. Johnson and Wigley, *Deconstructivist Architecture,* 19.
84. Johnson and Wigley, *Deconstructivist Architecture,* 19.
85. Johnson and Wigley, *Deconstructivist Architecture,* 17.
86. Johnson and Wigley, *Deconstructivist Architecture,* 19.
87. Johnson and Wigley, *Deconstructivist Architecture,* 19.
88. Kipnis, "Toward a New Architecture," 288.
89. Simondon, *Individuation in Light of Notions.*
90. Kwinter, *Far from Equilibrium,* 146.
91. Kwinter, *Far from Equilibrium,* 146.
92. Kwinter, *Far from Equilibrium,* 147.
93. Bruno, *Cause, Principle and Unity.*
94. See Harman, "Whitehead and Schools X, Y, and Z."
95. Kwinter, *Architectures of Time,* 10.
96. See DeLanda, *Intensive Science and Virtual Philosophy.*
97. Kwinter, *Architectures of Time,* 29–31.
98. Thom, *Structural Stability and Morphogenesis.*
99. Kwinter, *Architectures of Time,* 14.
100. Kwinter, *Architectures of Time,* 14.
101. DeLanda, in DeLanda and Harman, *The Rise of Realism,* 82.
102. Kwinter, *Architectures of Time,* 14.
103. See, for instance, Foucault, *Discipline and Punish.*
104. Allen, "From Object to Field," 24.
105. Allen, "From Object to Field," 28.
106. Allen, "From Object to Field," 29.
107. Rajchman, "Out of the Fold," 78.
108. Allen, "From Object to Field," 30.
109. Allen, "From Object to Field," 24–25.
110. Allen, "From Object to Field," 30.
111. Lynn, "Introduction," 9.
112. Lynn, "Architectural Curvilinearity," 24.
113. Lynn, "Introduction," 9. On complexity theory, see Kauffman, *The Origins of Order.*

114. Lynn, "Architectural Curvilinearity," 24.
115. Lynn, "Architectural Curvilinearity," 26.
116. Lynn, "Architectural Curvilinearity," 26.
117. Lynn, "Architectural Curvilinearity," 24.
118. Lynn, "Architectural Curvilinearity," 25.
119. Lynn, "Introduction," 9, 11 (intricacy); Lynn, "Architectural Curvilinearity," 30 (function).
120. Lynn, "Architectural Curvilinearity," 25, emphasis added.
121. Lynn, "Architectural Curvilinearity," 26.
122. Lynn, *Animate Form*, 11, 20 (Bergson), and 9 (ethic of stasis).
123. Lynn, *Animate Form*, 20.
124. Lynn, *Animate Form*, 35.
125. Lynn, *Animate Form*, 17.
126. Lynn, "Blobs, or Why Tectonics Is Square."
127. Lynn, *Animate Form*, 30.
128. Lynn, "Blobs, or Why Tectonics Is Square."
129. Lynn, *Animate Form*, 29.
130. Eisenman, *Written into the Void*, 2–5, in response to Derrida, 161–68 of the same volume.
131. Deleuze, *Negotiations*, 6.
132. For a brilliantly counterintuitive reading of Deleuze as a philosopher of individuals, see Kleinherenbrink, *Against Continuity*.
133. The references here are to Schumacher, *The Autopoiesis of Architecture*, to be discussed more directly in chapter 3.
134. Sloterdijk, *Spheres*: vol. 1, *Bubbles*; vol. 2, *Globes*; vol. 3, *Foam*.
135. Irigaray, *Speculum of the Other Woman*; Rawes, *Irigaray for Architects*.
136. Foucault, *Discipline and Punish*.
137. Norwood, "Metaphors for Nothing," 114–15.

2. I Know Not What

1. See Kruft, *A History of Architectural Theory*, chapters 1–2.
2. Alberti, *On the Art of Building in Ten Books*.
3. Laugier, *An Essay on Architecture*. The notion of the primitive hut was first discussed much earlier by the Renaissance Italian architect Filarete (born Antonio di Pietro Averlino), who credited no less a figure than Adam with its construction. See Filarete, *Filarete's Treatise on Architecture*. But unlike Laugier, Filarete did not view the primitive hut "as the norm of all architecture." See Kruft, *A History of Architectural Theory*, 52.
4. For the diligent newcomer to the field, one outstanding anthology of excerpts running from Vitruvius to the twenty-first

century is the two-volume *Architectural Theory*, edited by Harry Francis Mallgrave, joined by coeditor Christina Contandriopoulos in the second volume. Among the leading one-volume histories of architecture is Hanno-Walter Kruft's *A History of Architectural Theory from Vitruvius to the Present*, bearing in mind that in this case the "present" ends with Kruft's untimely death in 1993.

5. On the sublime, see especially Kant, *Critique of Judgment*; and Burke, *A Philosophical Enquiry*.

6. See Harman, "The Only Exit from Modern Philosophy."

7. Claude Perrault, annotations to his French translation of Vitruvius, *Les Dix Livres d'architecture de Vitruve*; Blondel, *Cours d'architecture*, vol. 2, part 3.

8. Serlio, *Sebastiano Serlio on Architecture*.

9. Fréart de Chantelou, *Diary of the Cavalière Bernini's Visit to Paris*, 7–9, 260–62. See also Burchard, "Bernini in Paris." Sigfried Giedion, however, gives the following alternative explanation: "Bernini failed to show a grasp of the complicated problems set by a palace building where women played an important role; he quite lost sight of the ladies." Giedion, *Space, Time and Architecture*, 134.

10. Palladio, *The Four Books of Architecture*.

11. Fischer, *Entwurff einer historischen Architektur*.

12. Boffrand, *Book of Architecture*; Quatremère de Quincy, *Enyclopédie méthodique*. On Boffrand's contribution, see Kruft, *A History of Architectural Theory*, 144–45.

13. Here I depart from the conclusions of Patrik Schumacher's useful discussion in volume 1 of *The Autopoiesis of Architecture*, 204ff.

14. Venturi, *Complexity and Contradiction in Architecture*; Aldo Rossi, *The Architecture of the City*.

15. Giedion, *Space, Time and Architecture*, 414.

16. De Zurko, *Origins of Functionalist Theory*, 4–5.

17. Lodoli, "Notes for a Projected Treatise on Architecture."

18. Bötticher, *Die Tektonik der Hellenen*.

19. Van der Nüll, "Andeutungen über die kunstgemäße Beziehung des Ornamentes zur rohen Form."

20. Semper, *Style in the Technical and Tectonic Arts*.

21. Wagner, *Modern Architecture*; Muthesius, *Style-Architecture and Building-Art*.

22. Reynaud, "Architecture"; Metzger, "Beitrag zur Zeitfrage"; Garbett, *Rudimentary Treatise on the Principles of Design*.

23. Sullivan, "The Tall Office Building Artistically Considered."

24. Greenough, *Form and Function*.

25. Sullivan, *System of Architectural Ornament*.

26. Le Roy, *Les Ruines des plus beaux monuments de la Grèce*; Piranesi, *Piranesi*.
27. See, for instance, Stern, *Architecture on the Edge of Postmodernism*.
28. See Sullivan, "Emotional Architecture as Compared with Intellectual."
29. A detailed prehistory can be found in De Zurko, *Origins of Functionalist Theory*.
30. Alberti, *On the Art of Building in Ten Books*, 7.
31. Maturana and Varela, *Autopoiesis and Cognition*.
32. For an example, see Brooks, *The Well Wrought Urn*. For a critique of this consequence of formalism, see Harman, "The Well-Wrought Broken Hammer."
33. See Greenberg, "The Pasted-Paper Revolution." For a critique of this insufficient modification of the flat background theory, see Harman, *Art and Objects*, 102–9.
34. Locke, *An Essay Concerning Human Understanding*.
35. Berkeley, *A Treatise Concerning the Principles of Human Knowledge*; Hume, *A Treatise of Human Nature*.
36. Heidegger, *Being and Time*; Derrida, *Of Grammatology*.
37. This is my primary criticism of Isabelle Stengers's generally fascinating multivolume work *Cosmopolitics*. See Harman, "Stengers on Emergence."
38. Nicholas of Cusa, "On Learned Ignorance."
39. See Harman, "The Third Table." In this respect I oppose the conceptual artist Joseph Kosuth. See Kosuth, "Art after Philosophy."
40. See Gadamer, *Truth and Method*, pt. 1, chap. 1. Gadamer is cited at the head of a helpful section on the *je ne sais quoi* in the history of art in Harrison, Wood, and Gaiger, *Art in Theory 1648–1815*, 205–38.
41. Gracián, *The Hero*, 143–45, also cited in Harrison, Wood, and Gaiger, *Art in Theory 1648–1815*, 207.
42. Leibniz, *Philosophical Papers and Letters*, 291, emphasis added.
43. Merleau-Ponty, *Phenomenology of Perception*, 79.
44. Mulhall, "How Complex Is a Lemon?" For my full response to Mulhall, see Harman, *Skirmishes*, 333–51.
45. Temple, "Upon the Gardens of Epicurus," 29–30, cited in Mallgrave, *Architectural Theory*, 230.
46. Chambers, *Designs of Chinese Buildings*, 14–18, cited in Mallgrave, *Architectural Theory*, 245.
47. Addison, "*The Spectator*, June 23, 1712," 593–95, 597–98, cited in Mallgrave, *Architectural Theory*, 234–39.
48. Kant, *Critique of Judgment*, 103.
49. Morton, *Hyperobjects*, 60. For further discussion, see Harman, "Hyperobjects and Prehistory."
50. Chalmers, *The Conscious Mind*.

51. Chalmers, *The Conscious Mind*, 293ff.
52. Dennett, *Consciousness Explained*.
53. Chalmers, *The Conscious Mind*, 94ff.
54. Another prominent author who sees consciousness as a very hard problem but underestimates the problem posed even by physical combination is Galen Strawson. See Strawson, "Realistic Monism."
55. Eddington, *The Nature of the Physical World*; Sellars, "Philosophy and the Scientific Image of Man."
56. Harman, "Zero-Person and the Psyche."
57. See Harman, "Heidegger, McLuhan and Schumacher."
58. For one treatment of the theme, see Trummer, "Zero Architecture."
59. Fried relates this story in "Art and Objecthood," 156.
60. Greenberg, "Review of Exhibitions," 6.
61. Eisenman, *Eisenman Inside Out*, 9. In recent years the original dissertation quoted here has itself been published under the title *The Formal Basis of Modern Architecture*.
62. Lynn, *Animate Form*, 35.
63. I am reminded by Mark Foster Gage that Burke approached an even more general insight when speaking of the way that beauty must be ascertained from just the right distance, which already implies a temporal process of trial and error. See Burke, *A Philosophical Enquiry*.
64. I leave for another occasion a dialogue with the possibly related notions of *eidos* and *morphe* in Aureli, *The Possibility of an Absolute Architecture*.
65. Rossi, *The Architecture of the City*, 46–48.
66. Rossi, *The Architecture of the City*, 41.
67. Rossi, *The Architecture of the City*, 46.
68. Rossi, *The Architecture of the City*, 47.
69. Rossi, *The Architecture of the City*, 55.
70. Rossi, *The Architecture of the City*, 61.
71. Rossi, *The Architecture of the City*, 113.
72. Rossi, *The Architecture of the City*, 126.

3. Object-Orientation

1. See Deleuze, *Logic of Sense*.
2. Schumacher, *The Autopoiesis of Architecture*, 297.
3. For a discussion of the various versions of Heidegger's fourfold, see Harman, *The Quadruple Object*.
4. Levinas, *Existence and Existents*.

5. This is the spirit of Benedikt's critique in *Architecture beyond Experience.*
6. Scharmen, Twitter thread, April 27, 2016.
7. Çelik Alexander, "Neo-naturalism," 24. For a defense of architecture against Hegel in particular, see Jarzombek, "A Conceptual Introduction to Architecture."
8. Brassier et al., "Speculative Realism."
9. Husserl, *Logical Investigations*; Heidegger, *Being and Time.*
10. See Hartmann, *Ontology.*
11. For a good recent account of his position, which is very different from OOO, see Ferraris, *Manifesto of New Realism.*
12. See, for instance, Harman, "Realism without Materialism."
13. Barad, *Meeting the Universe Halfway.* For a critique of Barad's interesting philosophical position, see Harman, "Agential and Speculative Realism."
14. See Harman, *Speculative Realism.* For correlationism, see Meillassoux, *After Finitude.* Niki Young, in his important article "On Correlationism and the Philosophy of (Human) Access," argues that I have been too quick to drop my own term "philosophy of human access" in favor of Meillassoux's "correlationism," and stresses a crucial difference between the two. I find Young's case persuasive.
15. See Harman, *Prince of Networks*; Harman, *Bruno Latour.*
16. For a more detailed treatment of this topic, see Harman, "The Only Exit from Modern Philosophy."
17. On the status of Hume, see Meillassoux, "Iteration, Reiteration, Repetition," 91n18.
18. Despite Meillassoux's urgent efforts to escape correlationism, he considers the correlationist argument against mainstream realism to be extremely powerful. See the often-overlooked "Presentation by Quentin Meillassoux" in Brassier et al., "Speculative Realism," 408–49.
19. Latour, *We Have Never Been Modern.*
20. Latour, *Pandora's Hope,* chap. 5; Latour, "On the Partial Existence of Existing *and* Nonexisting Objects."
21. Brassier, "Concepts and Objects," 64.
22. For a contrary view on Derrida, see Goldgaber, *Speculative Grammatology.*
23. Scharmen, Twitter thread, April 27, 2016.
24. Harman, *Weird Realism,* 8.
25. Wiscombe, "Discreteness."
26. See the cover image of Gage, *Projects and Provocations.*
27. Chambers, *Designs of Chinese Buildings,* 14–18, cited in Mallgrave, *Architectural Theory,* 245.

28. I owe this example to Simon Weir.
29. Lovecraft, *Tales*, 802.
30. Weir, "Object Oriented Ontology."
31. McLuhan and McLuhan, *Laws of Media*.
32. Harman, "The Revenge of the Surface."
33. Poe, *Essays and Reviews*, 1471.
34. Žižek, *The Parallax View*, 109.
35. Žižek, *The Parallax View*, 109.
36. Anderson, "Friedrich Nietzsche."
37. Nietzsche, *Twilight of the Idols*, 6.
38. Norwood, "Metaphors for Nothing," 115.
39. Bloom, *The Western Canon*, 11.
40. Lovecraft, *Tales*, 169.
41. Kipnis, "Toward a New Architecture," 315.
42. DeLanda, *A New Philosophy of Society*.
43. See the title chapter in Rowe, *The Mathematics of the Ideal Villa*, 2–27.
44. Derrida, in Eisenman, *Written into the Void*, 161.
45. Derrida, in Eisenman, *Written into the Void*, 162.
46. Eisenman, *Written into the Void*, 3.
47. Young, "The Aesthetics of Abstraction."
48. Deleuze, *Difference and Repetition*, xviii.

4. The Aesthetic Centrality of Architecture

1. The lecture was held under the aegis of a seminar series titled "The Matter of Contradiction: Ungrounding the Object."
2. Meillassoux, *After Finitude*.
3. Latour, "Why Has Critique Run Out of Steam?" In principle, Latour's "matters of concern" could be concerns for entities other than humans; in practice, Latour is less apt than his model, Alfred North Whitehead, to take this more cosmological turn.
4. Latour and Yaneva, "'Give Me a Gun and I Will Make Every Building Move.'" For a critical response, see Harman, "Buildings Are Not Processes."
5. Harman, *Guerrilla Metaphysics*.
6. Coggins, "Secret Powers."
7. Latour, *An Inquiry into Modes of Existence*.
8. Greenberg, *Homemade Esthetics*, 8ff.; Fried, "Art and Objecthood." For a discussion of Greenberg and Fried in relation to architecture, see Linder, *Nothing Less Than Literal*.
9. Harman, "On the Undermining of Objects"; Harman, "Undermining, Overmining, and Duomining."

10. Harman, "The Third Table."
11. Popper, *The Logic of Scientific Discovery*; Lakatos, "Changes in the Problem of Inductive Logic"; Bloom, *The Anxiety of Influence*. For a discussion of the relations among these three important but far-flung authors, see Harman, "On Progressive and Degenerating Research Programs."
12. Devitt, *Realism and Truth*, 347.
13. DeLanda, *A New Philosophy of Society*, 1.
14. Gibson, *The Ecological Approach to Visual Perception*.
15. Eyers, *Speculative Formalism*; Livingston, *The Politics of Logic*. For Gödel's famous proof, see Gödel, "On Formally Undecidable Propositions." The classic text of deconstruction is Derrida, *Of Grammatology*. One good source on the Lacanian Real is Lacan, *Anxiety*; Eyers offers a fine commentary on this topic in his *Lacan and the Problem of the "Real."* For Badiou's theory of the event as an excess of inclusion over belonging, see Badiou, *Being and Event*. On the topic of parallax, see Žižek, *The Parallax View*.
16. See Pippin, *After the Beautiful*.
17. Dante, *The Divine Comedy*.
18. Žižek, *The Sublime Object of Ideology*.
19. Aristotle, *Poetics*.
20. Brentano, *Psychology from an Empirical Standpoint*.
21. Luhmann, *Social Systems*; Luhmann, *Theory of Society*. The particular survey given here of the elements inside the cell has been gradually developed from its first presentation in Harman, "On Vicarious Causation."
22. Maturana and Varela, *Autopoiesis and Cognition*.
23. Dunham, Grant, and Watson, *Idealism*, 237. For my discussion of their interpretation, see Harman, *Speculative Realism*, 85–86.
24. Dunham, Grant, and Watson, *Idealism*, 227.
25. Dunham, Grant, and Watson, *Idealism*, 227–28.
26. Dunham, Grant, and Watson, *Idealism*, 234.
27. I will leave it for another occasion to consider Peter Sloterdijk's related meditations on "spheres." See Sloterdijk, *Spheres*, vols. 1–3.
28. See Harman, "Time, Space, Essence, and Eidos."
29. Schaffer, "Monism." Here I agree with the critique of Schaffer in Gabriel, *Why the World Does Not Exist*, and to that extent disagree with Tristan Garcia's brilliant book, *Form and Object*.
30. Leibniz, "The Principles of Philosophy."
31. Marías, *History of Philosophy*, 372.
32. McLuhan, *Understanding Media*. On retrieval and reversal, see McLuhan and McLuhan, *Laws of Media*.
33. Badiou, *Logics of Worlds*.

34. Heidegger, *On the Way to Language*.
35. Popper, *The Logic of Scientific Discovery*; Lakatos, *Philosophical Papers*; Kuhn, *The Structure of Scientific Revolutions*.
36. Brassier, *Nihil Unbound*.
37. McLuhan, *Understanding Media*.
38. Austin, *How to Do Things with Words*.
39. Badiou, *Being and Event*; Badiou, *Lacan*. The notion of an experience that "does not deceive" comes from Lacan's seminar on anxiety: Lacan, *Anxiety*.
40. Hume, *A Treatise of Human Nature*.
41. The recent hero of this approach, though not one of my own heroes, is Robert Brandom in his long book *Making It Explicit*.
42. Wolfendale, *Object-Oriented Philosophy*, 72.
43. See Harman, "A New Sense of Mimesis." There is some precedent here in the aesthetic theory of the German philosopher Theodor Lipps. See Lipps, *Ästhetik*, 2 vols.
44. Dunham, Grant, and Watson, *Idealism*, 234.
45. Kant, *Critique of Judgment*, 32.
46. Rancière, *The Emancipated Spectator*, 64.
47. Greenberg, *Homemade Esthetics*, 10–22.
48. Fried, *Manet's Modernism*.
49. Baudrillard, *Seduction*. See also Harman, "Object-Oriented Seduction."
50. Kant, *Critique of Judgment*, 73.
51. Derrida, "White Mythology."

5. The Architectural Cell

1. Hegel, *Phenomenology of Spirit*.
2. Dilthey, *The Formation of the Historical World*.
3. Darwin, *On the Origin of Species*.
4. Lyell, *Principles of Geology*.
5. Suger, *Selected Works of Abbot Suger*.
6. Görres, "Der Dom in Köln."
7. Viollet-le-Duc, "De la construction des édifices religieux."
8. Gage, "A Hospice for Parametricism," 131.
9. Hitchcock, *Modern Architecture*.
10. Wright, "The Cardboard House," 51.
11. Giedion, *Space, Time and Architecture*.
12. Mayne, *100 Buildings*, 10–13.
13. Le Corbusier, *Towards a New Architecture*, 4. This is just the first mention of the house-machine in the book; it reappears a number of times.

14. Giedion, *Space, Time and Architecture*, 580.
15. In a 1972 review of a New York show of Le Corbusier's art, Hilton Kramer writes as follows: "If the artist had produced nothing else in his life but his paintings and drawings of the Purist period, he would still merit a place (albeit a minor place) in the history of modern art." This seems like a prudent assessment of Corb's stature as an artist. Kramer, "Looking at Le Corbusier the Painter," 25.
16. Le Corbusier, *Towards a New Architecture*, 4, 7, 95, 107, 120, 227, 237, 240, 241, 263. Further page references to this book will appear in text in parentheses.
17. Heidegger, "Building Dwelling Thinking."
18. I have severely curtailed Le Corbusier's melodramatic use of italics and capitalization in this passage.
19. Heidegger, *The Question Concerning Technology*.
20. Here I have reversed the order of the two parts of the passage, in the interest of grammatical clarity.
21. Rowe, *The Mathematics of the Ideal Villa*, 8–9.
22. "The Spherical Solution." See also Giedion, *Time, Space and Architecture*, 676–88.
23. The quoted words come from Chandler's letter to Hamish Hamilton of October 6, 1946, in Chandler, *Raymond Chandler Speaking*, 217.
24. Harman, *Weird Realism*.
25. Kruft, *A History of Architectural Theory*, 446.
26. In this section, all page citations in parentheses refer to Eisenman, *Eisenman Inside Out*.
27. Tschumi, *Architecture and Disjunction*, 3.
28. Eisenman, *Written into the Void*, 4.
29. Eisenman, *Ten Canonical Buildings*, 53.
30. Heidegger, *Being and Time*.
31. For a defense of Aristotle's principle of identity against Derrida's somewhat threadbare accusations, see Harman, *Guerrilla Metaphysics*, 111–16. For a strong defense of Derrida's position, see Hägglund, *Radical Atheism*.
32. Eisenman, *Written into the Void*, 83.
33. Derrida, *Of Grammatology*, 22–23.
34. Eisenman, *Written into the Void*, 83.
35. Eisenman, *Written into the Void*, 121.
36. Fried, "Art and Objecthood."
37. Fried, "How Modernism Works"; Fried, "Anthony Caro's Table Sculptures."
38. See Gandelsonas and Morton, "On Reading Architecture." Graves had initially been Eisenman's ally in the "Whites" faction (see

Eisenman et al., *Five Architects*), as combated by the "Grays" (see Stern and Robertson, "Five on Five").

39. This will come as no surprise to anyone who has read Mark Linder's *Nothing Less Than Literal*, with its discussion of how formalist art criticism links minimalism with architecture.
40. Eisenman, *Written into the Void*, 4.
41. Eisenman, *Written into the Void*, 46.
42. Krauss, "A View of Modernism." For a critical assessment of Krauss's theoretical position, see Harman, *Art and Objects*, 124–30.
43. I make this case in my first book, *Tool-Being*.
44. For a more detailed treatment of this theme in connection with Heidegger, see Harman, *Tool-Being*, 63–66.
45. Kant does venture the negative rule that the disgusting can never be beautiful due to its inherently repellent character. Kant, *Critique of Judgment*, 180. But Charles Baudelaire and Georges Bataille immediately come to mind as striking counterexamples: authors who frequently manage to distill beauty even from initial disgust.
46. I owe these examples to Simon Weir.
47. Mayne, *100 Buildings*, 32–33.
48. Merleau-Ponty, *Phenomenology of Perception*, 79.
49. Johnson and Wigley, *Deconstructivist Architecture*, 19.
50. Kipnis, "Toward a New Architecture," 297.
51. Johnson and Wigley, *Deconstructivist Architecture*, 68.
52. Moore, "Zaha Hadid."
53. Schumacher, *The Autopoiesis of Architecture*.
54. Eisenman Architects, "Rebstockpark Masterplan."
55. Kipnis, "Toward a New Architecture," 292.
56. Kipnis, "Toward a New Architecture," 297.
57. Kipnis, "Toward a New Architecture," 297–98.
58. Bernard Tschumi Architects, "Le Fresnoy Arts Center."
59. Kipnis, "Toward a New Architecture," 298.
60. Kipnis, "Toward a New Architecture," 300.
61. Kipnis, "Recent Koolhaas," 117.
62. Kipnis, "Recent Koolhaas," 116.
63. Kipnis, "Recent Koolhaas," 120, 116.
64. Kipnis, "Recent Koolhaas," 137.
65. Kipnis, "Recent Koolhaas," 133.
66. Kipnis, "Recent Koolhaas," 135.
67. Kipnis, "Recent Koolhaas," 137.
68. See Steele and Koolhaas, *Supercritical*.
69. Hewitt, "Functionalist Paeans for Formalist Buildings."
70. Kipnis, "Recent Koolhaas," 117.

71. Kipnis, "Recent Koolhaas," 118.
72. Kipnis, "Recent Koolhaas," 117.
73. Kipnis, "Recent Koolhaas," 138.
74. Kipnis, "Recent Koolhaas," 116.
75. Kipnis, "Recent Koolhaas," 143.
76. Kipnis, "Recent Koolhaas," 143.
77. Kipnis, "Recent Koolhaas," 135, emphasis added.
78. Kipnis, "Recent Koolhaas," 126.
79. Kipnis, "Recent Koolhaas," 117.
80. For a consideration of Dalí that is at once architectural and object-oriented, see Simon Weir, "Salvador Dalí's Interiors with Heraclitus's Concealment."

BIBLIOGRAPHY

Addison, Joseph. "*The Spectator,* June 23, 1712." In *The Spectator.* London: George Routledge & Sons, 1868.

Alberti, Leon Battista. *On the Art of Building in Ten Books.* Translated by Joseph Rykwert, Neil Leach, and Robert Tavernor. Cambridge: MIT Press, 1991.

Allen, Stan. "From Object to Field." *Architectural Design* 67, nos. 5/6 (May/June 1997): 24–31.

Anderson, R. Lanier. "Friedrich Nietzsche." In *The Stanford Encyclopedia of Philosophy.* Summer 2017 ed. Edited by Edward N. Zalta. https://plato.stanford.edu.

Aristotle. *Metaphysics.* Translated by C. D. C. Reeve. Indianapolis: Hackett, 2016.

Aristotle. *Physics.* Translated by Robin Waterfield. Oxford: Oxford University Press, 2008.

Aristotle. *Poetics.* Translated by Joe Sachs. Newburyport, Mass.: Focus, 2006.

Aristotle. *The Rhetoric and Poetics of Aristotle.* Translated by Ingram Bywater. New York: Random House, 1984.

Aureli, Pier Vittorio. *The Possibility of an Absolute Architecture.* Cambridge: MIT Press, 2011.

Austin, J. L. *How to Do Things with Words.* 2nd ed. Cambridge, Mass.: Harvard University Press, 1975.

Aztlanquill. "An Element Called Oxygen." Allpoetry, circa 2011. https://allpoetry.com.

Bachelard, Gaston. *The Poetics of Space.* Translated by Maria Jolas. Boston: Beacon Press, 1994.

Badiou, Alain. *Being and Event.* Translated by Oliver Feltham. London: Continuum, 2005.

Badiou, Alain. *Lacan: Anti-philosophy 3.* Translated by Kenneth Reinhard and Susan Spitzer. New York: Columbia University Press, 2018.

Badiou, Alain. *Logics of Worlds: Being and Event II.* Translated by Alberto Toscano. London: Continuum, 2009.

Barad, Karen. *Meeting the Universe Halfway: Quantum Physics and the Entanglement of Matter and Meaning*. Durham, N.C.: Duke University Press, 2007.

Barthes, Roland. *Camera Lucida: Reflections on Photography*. Translated by Richard Howard. New York: Hill and Wang, 1982.

Baudrillard, Jean. *Seduction*. Translated by Brian Singer. New York: St. Martin's Press, 1990.

Benedikt, Michael. *Architecture beyond Experience*. San Francisco: Applied Research + Design Publishing, 2020.

Berkeley, George. *Alciphron; or, The Minute Philosopher*. In *The Works of George Berkeley D.D.*, 4 vols., edited by Alexander Campbell Fraser, 2:13–339. Oxford: Clarendon Press, 1871.

Berkeley, George. *A Treatise Concerning the Principles of Human Knowledge*. Indianapolis: Hackett, 1982.

Bernard Tschumi Architects. "Le Fresnoy Arts Center: Tourcoing, 1991–1997." http://www.tschumi.com.

Blondel, Jacques-François. *Cours d'architecture: Enseigné dans l'Academie Royale d'Architecture*. Paris: Academie Royale d'Architecture, 1675.

Bloom, Harold. *The Anxiety of Influence: A Theory of Poetry*. 2nd ed. Oxford: Oxford University Press, 2007.

Bloom, Harold. *The Western Canon: The Books and School of the Ages*. New York: Riverhead Books, 1994.

Boffrand, Germain. *Book of Architecture*. Edited by Caroline van Eck. Translated by David Britt. Burlington, Vt.: Ashgate, 2002.

Bötticher, Karl. *Die Tektonik der Hellenen*. Potsdam: Ferdinand Riegel, 1843.

Brandom, Robert B. *Making It Explicit: Reasoning, Representing, and Discursive Commitment*. Cambridge, Mass.: Harvard University Press, 1994.

Brassier, Ray. "Concepts and Objects." In *The Speculative Turn: Continental Materialism and Realism*, edited by Levi R. Bryant, Nick Srnicek, and Graham Harman, 47–65. Melbourne: re.press, 2011.

Brassier, Ray. *Nihil Unbound: Enlightenment and Extinction*. London: Palgrave Macmillan, 2007.

Brassier, Ray, Iain Hamilton Grant, Graham Harman, and Quentin Meillassoux. "Speculative Realism." *Collapse* 3 (2007): 307–450.

Brentano, Franz. *Psychology from an Empirical Standpoint*. Edited by Linda L. McAlister. Translated by Antos C. Rancurello, D. B. Terrell, and Linda L. McAlister. New York: Routledge, 1995.

Brooks, Cleanth. *The Well Wrought Urn: Studies in the Structure of Poetry*. New York: Harcourt, Brace and World, 1947.

Bruno, Giordano. *"Cause, Principle and Unity" and "Essays on Magic."* Translated and edited by Richard J. Blackwell and Robert de Lucca. Cambridge: Cambridge University Press, 1998.

Buber, Martin. *I and Thou.* Translated by Ronald Gregor Smith. Mansfield Centre, Conn.: Martino, 2010.

Burchard, Wolf. "Bernini in Paris: Architecture at a Crossroad." *Apollo,* April 13, 2015. https://www.apollo-magazine.com.

Burke, Edmund. *A Philosophical Enquiry into the Origin of Our Ideas of the Sublime and Beautiful.* Edited by Paul Guyer. Oxford: Oxford University Press, 2015.

Çelik Alexander, Zeynep. "Neo-naturalism." *Log,* no. 31 (Spring/Summer 2014): 23–30.

Chalmers, David. *The Conscious Mind: In Search of a Fundamental Theory.* Oxford: Oxford University Press, 1996.

Chambers, William. *Designs of Chinese Buildings, Furniture, Dresses, Machines, and Utensils.* New York: Benjamin Bloom, 1968.

Chandler, Raymond. *Raymond Chandler Speaking.* Edited by Dorothy Gardiner and Kathrine Sorley Walker. Berkeley: University of California Press, 1997.

Chomsky, Noam. *Cartesian Linguistics: A Chapter in the History of Rationalist Thought.* 3rd ed. Cambridge: Cambridge University Press, 2009.

Coggins, David. "Secret Powers: An Interview with Joanna Malinowska," *artnet,* January 24, 2010. http://www.artnet.com/magazineus/features/coggins/joanna-malinowska1-15-10.asp.

Dante Alighieri. *The Divine Comedy.* Translated by Allen Mandelbaum. New York: Random House, 1995.

Dante Alighieri. *La vita nuova.* Rev. ed. Translated by Barbara Reynolds. London: Penguin, 2004.

Darwin, Charles. *On the Origin of Species.* London: Penguin, 2009.

DeLanda, Manuel. *Intensive Science and Virtual Philosophy.* London: Continuum, 2002.

DeLanda, Manuel. *A New Philosophy of Society: Assemblage Theory and Social Complexity.* London: Continuum, 2006.

DeLanda, Manuel, and Graham Harman. *The Rise of Realism.* Cambridge: Polity Press, 2017.

Deleuze, Gilles. *Difference and Repetition.* Translated by Paul Patton. New York: Columbia University Press, 1995.

Deleuze, Gilles. *The Fold: Leibniz and the Baroque.* Translated by Tom Conley. Minneapolis: University of Minnesota Press, 1992.

Deleuze, Gilles. *Logic of Sense.* Translated by Mark Lester, with Charles Stivale. New York: Columbia University Press, 1990.

Deleuze, Gilles. *Negotiations 1972–1990.* Translated by Martin Joughin. New York: Columbia University Press, 1997.

Deleuze, Gilles, and Félix Guattari. *Anti-Oedipus: Capitalism and Schizophrenia.* Translated by Robert Hurley, Mark Seem, and Helen Lane. Minneapolis: University of Minnesota Press, 1983.

Deleuze, Gilles, and Félix Guattari. *A Thousand Plateaus: Capitalism and Schizophrenia.* Translated by Brian Massumi. Minneapolis: University of Minnesota Press, 1987.

Dennett, Daniel C. *Consciousness Explained.* Boston: Back Bay Books, 1992.

Derrida, Jacques. *Of Grammatology.* Translated by Gayatri Chakravorty Spivak. Baltimore: Johns Hopkins University Press, 1988.

Derrida, Jacques. "*Ousia* and *Gramme*: A Note on a Note from *Being and Time*." In *Margins of Philosophy*, translated by Alan Bass, 29–67. Chicago: University of Chicago Press, 1982.

Derrida, Jacques. "Point de folie—Maintenant l'architecture." Translated by Kate Linker. In Hays, *Architecture Theory since 1968,* 566–81.

Derrida, Jacques. "White Mythology: Metaphor in the Text of Philosophy." In *Margins of Philosophy*, translated by Alan Bass, 207–71. Chicago: University of Chicago Press, 1982.

Derrida, Jacques, and Peter Eisenman. *Chora L Works: Jacques Derrida and Peter Eisenman.* New York: Monacelli Press, 1997.

Devitt, Michael. *Realism and Truth.* 2nd ed. Princeton, N.J.: Princeton University Press, 1997.

De Zurko, Edward Robert. *Origins of Functionalist Theory.* New York: Columbia University Press, 1957.

Dilthey, Wilhelm. *The Formation of the Historical World in the Human Sciences.* Edited by Rudolf A. Makkreel and Frithjof Rodi. Princeton, N.J.: Princeton University Press, 2002.

Dunham, Jeremy, Iain Hamilton Grant, and Sean Watson. *Idealism: The History of a Philosophy.* Montreal: McGill-Queen's University Press, 2011.

Eddington, A. S. *The Nature of the Physical World.* New York: Macmillan, 1928.

Eisenman, Peter. *Eisenman Inside Out: Selected Writings, 1963–1988.* New Haven, Conn.: Yale University Press, 2004.

Eisenman, Peter. *The Formal Basis of Modern Architecture.* Zurich: Lars Müller, 2018.

Eisenman, Peter. *Ten Canonical Buildings: 1950–2000.* New York: Rizzoli, 2008.

Eisenman, Peter. *Written into the Void: Selected Writings, 1990–2004.* New Haven, Conn.: Yale University Press, 2011.

Eisenman, Peter, Michael Graves, Charles Gwathmey, John Hejduk, and Richard Meier. *Five Architects.* New York: Wittenborn, 1972.

Eisenman Architects. "Rebstockpark Masterplan." 1992. https://eisenmanarchitects.com.

Eyers, Tom. *Lacan and the Problem of the "Real."* London: Palgrave Macmillan, 2012.

Eyers, Tom. *Speculative Formalism: Literature, Theory, and the Critical Present.* Evanston, Ill.: Northwestern University Press, 2017.

Ferraris, Maurizio. *Manifesto of New Realism.* Translated by Sarah De Sanctis. Albany: State University of New York Press, 2014.

Filarete [Antonio di Pietro Averlino]. *Filarete's Treatise on Architecture.* Vol. 2. Translated by John R. Spencer. New Haven, Conn.: Yale University Press, 1965.

Fischer von Erlach, Johann Bernhard. *Entwurff einer historischen Architektur.* Vienna, 1721.

Foucault, Michel. *Discipline and Punish: The Birth of the Prison.* 2nd ed. Translated by Alan Sheridan. New York: Vintage, 1991.

Fréart de Chantelou, Paul. *Diary of the Cavalière Bernini's Visit to Paris.* Edited by Anthony Blunt. Translated by Margery Corbett. Princeton, N.J.: Princeton University Press, 1985.

Fried, Michael. "Anthony Caro's Table Sculptures, 1966–77." In *Art and Objecthood: Essays and Reviews,* 202–12. Chicago: University of Chicago Press, 1998.

Fried, Michael. "Art and Objecthood." In *Art and Objecthood: Essays and Reviews,* 148–72. Chicago: University of Chicago Press, 1998.

Fried, Michael. "How Modernism Works: A Response to T. J. Clark." In *Pollock and After: The Critical Debate,* 2nd ed., edited by Francis Fracina, 87–101. New York: Routledge, 2000.

Fried, Michael. *Manet's Modernism; or, The Face of Painting in the 1860s.* Chicago: University of Chicago Press, 1996.

Gabriel, Markus. *Why the World Does Not Exist.* Translated by Gregory Moss. Cambridge: Polity Press, 2017.

Gadamer, Hans-Georg. *Truth and Method.* 2nd rev. ed. Translation revised by Joel Weinsheimer and Donald G. Marshall. London: Continuum, 1989.

Gage, Mark Foster, ed. *Aesthetics Equals Politics: New Discourses across Art, Architecture, and Philosophy.* Cambridge: MIT Press, 2019.

Gage, Mark Foster. "A Hospice for Parametricism." *Architectural Design* 86, no. 2 (March 2016): 128–33.

Gage, Mark Foster. *Projects and Provocations.* New York: Rizzoli, 2018.

Gandelsonas, Mario, and David Morton. "On Reading Architecture." *Progressive Architecture,* March 1972.

Gannon, Todd, Graham Harman, David Ruy, and Tom Wiscombe. "The Object Turn: A Conversation." *Log,* no. 33 (Winter 2015): 73–94.

Garbett, Edward Lacy. *Rudimentary Treatise on the Principles of Design in Architecture, as Deducible from Nature and Exemplified in the Works of the Greek and Gothic Architects.* London: J. Weale, 1850.

Garcia, Tristan. *Form and Object: A Treatise on Things.* Translated by

Mark Allan Ohm and Jon Cogburn. Edinburgh: Edinburgh University Press, 2014.

Gibson, James J. *The Ecological Approach to Visual Perception.* London: Routledge, 2014.

Giedion, Sigfried. *Space, Time and Architecture: The Growth of a New Tradition.* 5th ed., rev. and enlarged. Cambridge, Mass.: Harvard University Press, 1977.

Gödel, Kurt. "On Formally Undecidable Propositions of the *Principia Mathematica* and Related Systems. I." In *The Undecidable: Basic Papers on Undecidable Propositions, Unsolvable Problems and Computable Functions,* edited by Martin Davis, 4–38. Mineola, N.Y.: Dover, 2004.

Goldgaber, Deborah. *Speculative Grammatology: Deconstruction and the New Materialism.* Edinburgh: Edinburgh University Press, 2020.

Görres, Joseph. "Der Dom in Köln." *Rheinischer Merkur,* November 20, 1814.

Gracián, Baltasar. *The Art of Worldly Wisdom: A Pocket Oracle.* Translated by Christopher Maurer. New York: Doubleday, 1992.

Gracián, Baltasar. *The Hero.* Translated by J. de Courbeville. London: T. Cox, 1726.

Greenberg, Clement. *Homemade Esthetics: Observations on Art and Taste.* Oxford: Oxford University Press, 1999.

Greenberg, Clement. "The Pasted-Paper Revolution." In *The Collected Essays and Criticism.* Vol. 4, *Modernism with a Vengeance, 1957–1969,* 61–66. Chicago: University of Chicago Press, 1995.

Greenberg, Clement. "Review of Exhibitions of Edgar Degas and Richard Pousette-Dart." In *The Collected Essays and Criticism.* Vol. 2, *Arrogant Purpose, 1945–1949,* 6–7. Chicago: University of Chicago Press, 1988.

Greenough, Horatio. *Form and Function: Remarks on Art, Design, and Architecture.* Berkeley: University of California Press, 1947.

Gropius, Walter. *Scope of Total Architecture.* New York: Collier Books, 1955.

Hägglund, Martin. *Radical Atheism: Derrida and the Time of Life.* Stanford, Calif.: Stanford University Press, 2008.

Harman, Graham. "Aesthetics as First Philosophy: Levinas and the Non-human." *Naked Punch* 9 (Summer/Fall 2007): 21–30.

Harman, Graham. "Agential and Speculative Realism: Remarks on Barad's Ontology." *Rhizomes,* no. 30 (2016). http://www.rhizomes.net.

Harman, Graham. *Art and Objects.* Cambridge: Polity Press, 2020.

Harman, Graham. *Bruno Latour: Reassembling the Political.* London: Pluto, 2014.

Harman, Graham. "Buildings Are Not Processes: A Disagreement with Latour and Yaneva." *Ardeth* 1 (2017): 113–22.

Harman, Graham. *Dante's Broken Hammer: The Ethics, Aesthetics, and Metaphysics of Love.* London: Repeater, 2016.

Harman, Graham. "Dwelling with the Fourfold." *Space and Culture* 12, no. 3 (2009): 292–302.

Harman, Graham. *Guerrilla Metaphysics: Phenomenology and the Carpentry of Things.* Chicago: Open Court, 2005.

Harman, Graham. "Heidegger, McLuhan and Schumacher on Form and Its Aliens." *Theory, Culture & Society* 33, no. 6 (2016): 99–105.

Harman, Graham. "Hyperobjects and Prehistory." In *Time and History in Prehistory,* edited by Stella Souvatzi, Adnan Baysal, and Emma L. Baysal, 195–209. London: Routledge, 2019.

Harman, Graham. "A New Sense of Mimesis." In Gage, *Aesthetics Equals Politics,* 49–63.

Harman, Graham. "Object-Oriented Seduction: Baudrillard Reconsidered." In *The War of Appearances: Transparency, Opacity, Radiance,* edited by Joke Brouwer, Lars Spuybroek, and Sjoerd van Tuinen, 128–43. Amsterdam: Sonic Acts Press, 2016.

Harman, Graham. "Objects and Orientalism." In *The Agon of Interpretations: Towards a Critical Intercultural Hermeneutics,* edited by Ming Xie, 123–39. Toronto: University of Toronto Press, 2014.

Harman, Graham. "The Only Exit from Modern Philosophy." *Open Philosophy* 3 (2020): 132–46.

Harman, Graham. "On Progressive and Degenerating Research Programs with Respect to Philosophy." *Revista Portuguesa de Filosofia* 75, no. 4 (2019): 2473–2508.

Harman, Graham. "On the Undermining of Objects: Grant, Bruno, and Radical Philosophy." In *The Speculative Turn: Continental Materialism and Realism,* edited by Levi R. Bryant, Nick Srnicek, and Graham Harman, 21–40. Melbourne: re.press, 2011.

Harman, Graham. "On Vicarious Causation." *Collapse* 2 (2007): 171–205.

Harman, Graham. *Prince of Networks: Bruno Latour and Metaphysics.* Melbourne: re.press, 2009.

Harman, Graham. *The Quadruple Object.* Winchester, England: Zero Books, 2011.

Harman, Graham. "Realism without Materialism." *SubStance* 40, no. 2 (2011): 52–72.

Harman, Graham. "The Revenge of the Surface: Heidegger, McLuhan, Greenberg." *Paletten,* nos. 291/292 (2013): 66–73.

Harman, Graham. *Skirmishes: With Friends, Enemies, and Neutrals.* Brooklyn, N.Y.: punctum books, 2020.

Harman, Graham. *Speculative Realism: An Introduction.* Cambridge: Polity Press, 2018.

Harman, Graham. "Stengers on Emergence." *BioSocieties* 9, no. 1 (March 2014): 99–104.

Harman, Graham. "The Third Table." In *The Book of Books,* edited by Carolyn Christov-Bakargiev, 540–42. Ostfildern, Germany: Hatje Cantz, 2012.

Harman, Graham. "Time, Space, Essence, and Eidos: A New Theory of Causation." *Cosmos and History* 6, no. 1 (2010): 1–17.

Harman, Graham. *Tool-Being: Heidegger and the Metaphysics of Objects.* Chicago: Open Court, 2002.

Harman, Graham. "Undermining, Overmining, and Duomining: A Critique." In *ADD Metaphysics,* edited by Jenna Sutela, 40–51. Espoo, Finland: Aalto University Design Research Laboratory, 2013.

Harman, Graham. *Weird Realism: Lovecraft and Philosophy.* Winchester, England: Zero Books, 2012.

Harman, Graham. "The Well-Wrought Broken Hammer: Object-Oriented Literary Criticism." *New Literary History* 43, no. 2 (Spring 2012): 183–203.

Harman, Graham. "Whitehead and Schools X, Y, and Z." In *The Lure of Whitehead,* edited by Nicholas Gaskill and A. J. Nocek, 231–48. Minneapolis: University of Minnesota Press, 2014.

Harman, Graham. "Zero-Person and the Psyche." In *Mind That Abides: Panpsychism in the New Millennium,* edited by David Skrbina, 253–82. Amsterdam: John Benjamins, 2009.

Harrison, Charles, Paul Wood, and Jason Gaiger, eds. *Art in Theory 1648–1815: An Anthology of Changing Ideas.* Oxford: Blackwell, 2000.

Hartmann, Nicolai. *Ontology: Laying the Foundations.* Berlin: De Gruyter, 2019.

Hays, K. Michael, ed. *Architecture Theory since 1968.* Cambridge: MIT Press, 2000.

Hegel, G. W. F. *Phenomenology of Spirit.* Translated by A. V. Miller. Oxford: Oxford University Press, 1977.

Heidegger, Martin. *Being and Time.* Translated by John Macquarrie and Edward Robinson. New York: Harper, 1962.

Heidegger, Martin. "Building Dwelling Thinking." In *Basic Writings: Ten Key Essays, plus the Introduction to "Being and Time,"* edited by David Farrell Krell, 347–63. New York: HarperCollins, 1993.

Heidegger, Martin. *Country Path Conversations.* Translated by Bret W. Davis. Bloomington: Indiana University Press, 2010.

Heidegger, Martin. "Insight into That Which Is." In *Bremen and Freiburg Lectures,* translated by Andrew J. Mitchell, 1–76. Bloomington: Indiana University Press, 2012.

Heidegger, Martin. *On the Way to Language.* Translated by Peter D. Hertz. San Francisco: Harper, 1971.

Heidegger, Martin. *The Question Concerning Technology, and Other Essays.* Translated by William Lovitt. New York: Harper & Row, 1977.

Heidegger, Martin. "The Thing." In *Poetry, Language, Thought,* translated by Albert Hofstadter, 161–84. New York: Harper, 1971.

Hewitt, Mark Alan. "Functionalist Paeans for Formalist Buildings." Common Edge, June 4, 2019. https://commonedge.org.

Hitchcock, Henry-Russell. *Modern Architecture: Romanticism and Reintegration.* New York: Hacker Art Books, 1970.

Hume, David. *A Treatise of Human Nature.* Oxford: Oxford University Press, 1978.

Husserl, Edmund. *Logical Investigations.* 2 vols. Translated by J. N. Findlay. London: Routledge & Kegan Paul, 1970.

Ingraham, Catherine. "The Burdens of Linearity: Donkey Urbanism." In Hays, *Architecture Theory since 1968,* 644–57.

Ingraham, Catherine. "Milking Deconstruction, *or* Cow Was the Show?" Excerpt in Mallgrave and Contandriopoulos, *Architectural Theory,* 479–80.

Irigaray, Luce. *Speculum of the Other Woman.* Translated by Gillian C. Gill. Ithaca, N.Y.: Cornell University Press, 1985.

Jarzombek, Mark. "A Conceptual Introduction to Architecture." *Log,* no. 15 (Winter 2009): 89–98.

Johnson, Philip, and Mark Wigley. *Deconstructivist Architecture.* New York: Museum of Modern Art, 1988.

Kant, Immanuel. *Critique of Judgment.* Translated by Werner S. Pluhar. Indianapolis: Hackett, 1987.

Kant, Immanuel. *Critique of Practical Reason.* Translated by Mary Gregor. Cambridge: Cambridge University Press, 2015.

Kant, Immanuel. *Critique of Pure Reason.* Translated by Werner S. Pluhar. Indianapolis: Hackett, 1996.

Kauffman, Stuart A. *The Origins of Order: Self-Organization and Selection in Evolution.* Oxford: Oxford University Press, 2000.

Kaufmann, Emil. *Von Ledoux bis Le Corbusier, Ursprung und Entwicklung der autonomen Architektur.* Vienna: Rolf Passer, 1933.

Kipnis, Jeffrey. "Recent Koolhaas." In *A Question of Qualities: Essays in Architecture,* 115–45. Cambridge: MIT Press, 2013.

Kipnis, Jeffrey. "Toward a New Architecture." In *A Question of Qualities: Essays in Architecture,* 287–323. Cambridge: MIT Press, 2013.

Kleinherenbrink, Arjen. *Against Continuity: Gilles Deleuze's Speculative Realism.* Edinburgh: Edinburgh University Press, 2019.

Kosuth, Joseph. "Art after Philosophy/Kunst nach der Philosophie," first part. Translated by W. Höck. In *Art and Language,* edited by Paul Maenz and Gerd de Vries, 74–99. Cologne: M. DuMont Schauberg, 1972.

Kramer, Hilton. "Looking at Le Corbusier the Painter." *New York Times,* January 29, 1972, 25.

Krauss, Rosalind. "A View of Modernism." *Artforum*, September 1972, 48–51. https://www.artforum.com.

Kruft, Hanno-Walter. *A History of Architectural Theory from Vitruvius to the Present.* Translated by Ronald Taylor, Elsie Callander, and Antony Wood. London: Zwemmer, 1994.

Kuhn, Thomas. *The Structure of Scientific Revolutions.* 3rd ed. Chicago: University of Chicago Press, 1996.

Kwinter, Sanford. *Architectures of Time: Toward a Theory of the Event in Modernist Culture.* Cambridge: MIT Press, 2002.

Kwinter, Sanford. *Far from Equilibrium: Essays on Technology and Design Culture.* Barcelona: Actar, 2008.

Lacan, Jacques. *Anxiety: The Seminar of Jacques Lacan, Book X.* Edited by Jacques-Alain Miller. Translated by Adrian Price. Cambridge: Polity Press, 2016.

Lakatos, Imre. "Changes in the Problem of Inductive Logic." In *Philosophical Papers.* Vol. 2, *Mathematics, Science, and Epistemology*, 128–200. Cambridge: Cambridge University Press, 1978.

Lakatos, Imre. *Philosophical Papers.* Vol. 1, *The Methodology of Scientific Research Programs.* Cambridge: Cambridge University Press, 1978.

Latour, Bruno. *An Inquiry into Modes of Existence: An Anthropology of the Moderns.* Translated by Catherine Porter. Cambridge, Mass.: Harvard University Press, 2013.

Latour, Bruno. "On the Partial Existence of Existing and Nonexisting Objects." In *Biographies of Scientific Objects*, edited by Lorraine Daston, 247–69. Chicago: University of Chicago Press, 2000.

Latour, Bruno. *Pandora's Hope: Essays on the Reality of Science Studies.* Cambridge, Mass.: Harvard University Press, 1999.

Latour, Bruno. *Reassembling the Social: An Introduction to Actor-Network-Theory.* Oxford: Oxford University Press, 2007.

Latour, Bruno. *We Have Never Been Modern.* Translated by Catherine Porter. Cambridge, Mass.: Harvard University Press, 1993.

Latour, Bruno. "Why Has Critique Run Out of Steam? From Matters of Fact to Matters of Concern." *Critical Inquiry* 30, no. 2 (Winter 2004): 225–48.

Latour, Bruno, and Albena Yaneva. "'Give Me a Gun and I Will Make Every Building Move': An Ant's View of Architecture." In *Explorations in Architecture: Teaching, Design, Research*, edited by Reto Geiser, 80–89. Basel: Birkhäuser, 2008.

Laugier, Marc-Antoine. *An Essay on Architecture.* Translated by Wolfgang Herrmann and Anni Herrmann. Los Angeles: Hennessey & Ingalls, 2009.

Le Corbusier [Charles-Édouard Jeanneret]. *Towards a New Architecture.* Translated by Frederick Etchells. New York: Dover, 1986.

Leibniz, G. W. *Philosophical Papers and Letters: A Selection.* Translated by Leroy E. Loemker. Dordrecht: Springer, 2012.

Leibniz, G. W. "The Principles of Philosophy, or, the Monadology." In *Philosophical Essays,* translated and edited by Roger Ariew and Daniel Garber, 213–25. Indianapolis: Hackett, 1989.

Le Roy, Julien-David. *Les Ruines des plus beaux monuments de la Grèce.* Paris: H. L. Guerin & L. F. Delatour, 1758.

Levinas, Emmanuel. *Existence and Existents.* Translated by Alphonso Lingis. Pittsburgh: Duquesne University Press, 2001.

Levine, Caroline. *Forms: Whole, Rhythm, Hierarchy, Network.* Princeton, N.J.: Princeton University Press, 2017.

Linder, Mark. *Nothing Less Than Literal: Architecture after Minimalism.* Cambridge: MIT Press, 2004.

Lipps, Theodor. *Ästhetik: Psychologie des schönen und der Kunst, Erster Teil: Grundlegung der Ästhetik.* Hamburg: Leopold Voss, 1903.

Lipps, Theodor. *Ästhetik: Psychologie des schönen und der Kunst, Zweiter Teil.* Hamburg: Leopold Voss, 1920.

Livingston, Paul. *The Politics of Logic: Badiou, Wittgenstein, and the Consequences of Formalism.* London: Routledge, 2011.

Locke, John. *An Essay Concerning Human Understanding.* 2 vols. Mineola, N.Y.: Dover, 1959.

Lodoli, Carlo. "Notes for a Projected Treatise on Architecture." Translated by Edgar Kaufmann Jr. *Art Bulletin* 46, no. 1 (March 1964): 162–64.

Loos, Adolf. "Ornament and Crime." In *Ornament and Crime: Selected Essays,* translated by Michael Mitchell. Riverside, Calif.: Ariadne Press, 1997.

Lovecraft, H. P. *Tales.* New York: Library of America, 2005.

Luhmann, Niklas. *Social Systems.* Translated by John Bednarz Jr., with Dirk Baecker. Stanford, Calif.: Stanford University Press, 1996.

Luhmann, Niklas. *Theory of Society.* 2 vols. Translated by Rhodes Barrett. Stanford, Calif.: Stanford University Press, 2012–13.

Lyell, Charles. *Principles of Geology.* London: Penguin, 1998.

Lynn, Greg. *Animate Form.* New York: Princeton Architectural Press, 1999.

Lynn, Greg. "Architectural Curvilinearity: The Folded, the Pliant, and the Supple." In Lynn, *Folding in Architecture,* 24–31.

Lynn, Greg. "Blobs, or Why Tectonics Is Square and Topology Is Groovy." *ANY: Architecture New York,* no. 14 (1996): 58–61.

Lynn, Greg, ed. *Folding in Architecture.* London: John Wiley, 2004.

Lynn, Greg. "Introduction." In Lynn, *Folding in Architecture,* 9–12.

Mallgrave, Harry Francis, ed. *Architectural Theory.* Vol. 1, *An Anthology from Vitruvius to 1870.* Oxford: Blackwell, 2006.

Mallgrave, Harry Francis, and Christina Contandriopoulos, eds.

Architectural Theory. Vol. 2, *An Anthology from 1871 to 2005.* Oxford: Blackwell, 2008.

Marías, Julián. *History of Philosophy.* Translated by Stanley Appelbaum and Clarence C. Strowbridge. New York: Dover, 1967.

Maturana, Humberto, and Francisco Varela. *Autopoiesis and Cognition: The Realization of the Living.* Dordrecht: D. Reidel, 1980.

Mayne, Thom, ed. *100 Buildings.* New York: Rizzoli, 2017.

McLuhan, Marshall. *Understanding Media: The Extensions of Man.* Cambridge: MIT Press, 1994.

McLuhan, Marshall, and Eric McLuhan. *Laws of Media: The New Science.* Toronto: University of Toronto Press, 1992.

Meillassoux, Quentin. *After Finitude: An Essay on the Necessity of Contingency.* Translated by Ray Brassier. London: Continuum, 2008.

Meillassoux, Quentin. "Iteration, Reiteration, Repetition: A Speculative Analysis of the Sign Devoid of Meaning." Translated by Robin Mackay and Moritz Gansen. In *Genealogies of Speculation: Materialism and Subjectivity since Structuralism,* edited by Armen Avanessian and Suhail Malik, 117–97. London: Bloomsbury, 2016.

Merleau-Ponty, Maurice. *Phenomenology of Perception.* Translated by Colin Smith. London: Routledge, 2002.

Metzger, Eduard. "Beitrag zur Zeitfrage: In welchem Stil man bauen soll!" *Allgemeine Bauzeitung* 10 (1845).

Moore, Rowan. "Zaha Hadid: Queen of the Curve." *The Guardian,* September 7, 2013. https://www.theguardian.com.

Morgan, Diane. *Kant for Architects.* London: Routledge, 2017.

Morton, Timothy. *Hyperobjects: Philosophy and Ecology after the End of the World.* Minneapolis: University of Minnesota Press, 2013.

Mulhall, Stephen. "How Complex Is a Lemon?" *London Review of Books* 40, no. 18 (September 27, 2018). https://www.lrb.co.uk.

Muthesius, Hermann. *Style-Architecture and Building-Art: Transformations of Architecture in the Nineteenth Century and Its Present Condition.* Santa Monica, Calif.: Getty Center for the History of Art and the Humanities, 1994.

Nicholas of Cusa. "On Learned Ignorance." In *Selected Spiritual Writings,* 85–206. Mahwah, N.J.: Paulist Press.

Nietzsche, Friedrich. *Twilight of the Idols.* Translated by Richard Polt. Indianapolis: Hackett, 1997.

Norberg-Schulz, Christian. *Genius Loci: Towards a Phenomenology of Architecture.* New York: Rizzoli, 1979.

Norwood, Bryan E. "Metaphors for Nothing." *Log,* no. 33 (Winter 2015): 107–19.

Palladio, Andrea. *The Four Books of Architecture.* Translated by Adolf K. Placzek. Mineola, N.Y.: Dover, 1965.

Pallasmaa, Juhani. *The Eyes of the Skin: Architecture and the Senses.* Chichester: John Wiley, 2005.

Pippin, Robert B. *After the Beautiful: Hegel and the Philosophy of Pictorial Modernism.* Chicago: University of Chicago Press, 2014.

Piranesi, Giovanni Battista. *Piranesi: The Complete Etchings.* 2 vols. Edited by John Wilton-Ely. San Francisco: Alan Wofsy Fine Arts, 1994.

Plato. "Timaeus." In *Timaeus and Critias,* translated by Robin Waterfield, 1–99. Oxford: Oxford University Press, 2008.

Poe, Edgar Allan. *Essays and Reviews.* New York: Library of America, 1984.

Popper, Karl. *The Logic of Scientific Discovery.* London: Routledge, 1992.

Pugin, A. W. N. *The True Principles of Pointed or Christian Architecture.* London: Academy Editions, 1973.

Quatremère de Quincy, A.-C. *Encyclopédie méthodique: Architecture.* Paris: Panckouke, 1788.

Rajchman, John. "Out of the Fold." In Lynn, *Folding in Architecture,* 77–79.

Rancière, Jacques. *The Emancipated Spectator.* Translated by Gregory Elliott. London: Verso, 2011.

Rand, Ayn. *The Fountainhead.* New York: Signet, 1996.

Rawes, Peg. *Irigaray for Architects.* London: Routledge, 2007.

Reynaud, Léonce. "Architecture." In *Encyclopédie nouvelle.* Geneva: Slatkine Reprints, 1991.

Rossi, Aldo. *The Architecture of the City.* Translated by Diane Ghirardo and Joan Ockman. Cambridge: MIT Press, 1982.

Rowe, Colin. *The Mathematics of the Ideal Villa and Other Essays.* Cambridge: MIT Press, 1976.

Ruskin, John. *The Seven Lamps of Architecture.* Mineola, N.Y.: Dover, 1989.

Ruy, David. "Returning to (Strange) Objects." *tarp: Architecture Manual,* no. 10 (Spring 2012): 38–42.

Said, Edward. *Orientalism.* New York: Vintage Books, 1979.

Schaffer, Jonathan. "Monism: The Priority of the Whole." *Philosophical Review* 119, no. 1 (2010): 31–76.

Schumacher, Patrik. *The Autopoiesis of Architecture.* Vol. 1, *A New Framework for Architecture.* London: John Wiley, 2011.

Sellars, Wilfrid. "Philosophy and the Scientific Image of Man." In *In the Space of Reasons,* 369–408. Cambridge, Mass.: Harvard University Press, 2007.

Semper, Gottfried. *Style in the Technical and Tectonic Arts; or, Practical Aesthetics.* Translated by Harry Francis Mallgrave and Michael Robinson. Los Angeles: Getty Publications, 2004.

Serlio, Sebastiano. *Sebastiano Serlio on Architecture.* Vol. 1. Translated by Vaughan Hart and Peter Hicks. New Haven, Conn.: Yale University Press, 2005.

Sharr, Adam. *Heidegger for Architects.* London: Routledge, 2007.

Shklovsky, Viktor. *Theory of Prose.* Translated by Benjamin Sher. Normal, Ill.: Dalkey Archive Press, 1991.

Simondon, Gilbert. *Individuation in Light of Notions of Form and Information.* 2 vols. Translated by Taylor Adkins. Minneapolis: University of Minnesota Press, 2020.

Sloterdijk, Peter. *Spheres.* Vol. 1, *Bubbles.* Translated by Wieland Hoban. New York: Semiotext(e), 2011.

Sloterdijk, Peter. *Spheres.* Vol. 2, *Globes.* Translated by Wieland Hoban. New York: Semiotext(e), 2014.

Sloterdijk, Peter. *Spheres.* Vol. 3, *Foam.* Translated by Wieland Hoban. New York: Semiotext(e), 2016.

"The Spherical Solution." Sydney Opera House website. Accessed March 9, 2020. https://www.sydneyoperahouse.com.

Steele, Brett, Peter Eisenman, and Rem Koolhaas. *Supercritical: Peter Eisenman Meets Rem Koolhaas.* London: AA Publications, 2007.

Stengers, Isabelle. *Cosmopolitics.* 2 vols. Translated by Robert Bononno. Minneapolis: University of Minnesota Press, 2010.

Stern, Robert A. M. *Architecture on the Edge of Postmodernism: Collected Essays 1964–1988.* New Haven, Conn.: Yale University Press, 2009.

Stern, Robert A. M., and Jaquelin Robertson. "Five on Five." *Architectural Forum* 138, no. 4 (May 1973): 46–53.

Strawson, Galen. "Realistic Monism: Why Physicalism Entails Panpsychism." *Journal of Consciousness Studies* 13, nos. 10/11 (2006): 3–31.

Suger, Abbot. *Selected Works of Abbot Suger of Saint-Denis.* Translated by Richard Cusimano and Eric Whitmore. Washington, D.C.: Catholic University of America Press, 2018.

Sullivan, Louis. "Emotional Architecture as Compared with Intellectual: A Study in Subjective and Objective." *Inland Architect and News Record* 24, no. 4 (November 1894).

Sullivan, Louis. *System of Architectural Ornament.* New York: Eakins Press Foundation, 1968.

Sullivan, Louis. "The Tall Office Building Artistically Considered." In *Kindergarten Chats and Other Writings,* 202–13. Eastford, Conn.: Martino Fine Books, 2014.

Tafuri, Manfredo. *Theories and History of Architecture.* Translated by Giorgio Verrecchia. New York: Harper & Row, 1980.

Temple, William. "Upon the Gardens of Epicurus; or, Of Gardening, in the Year 1685." In *Five Miscellaneous Essays by Sir William Temple,* edited by Samuel Holt Monk, 1–36. Ann Arbor: University of Michigan Press, 1963.

Thom, René. *Structural Stability and Morphogenesis.* New York: Basic Books, 1989.

Trummer, Peter. "Zero Architecture: A Neorealist Approach to the Architecture of the City." *SAC Journal* 5 (2019): 12–19.

Tschumi, Bernard. *Architecture and Disjunction.* Cambridge: MIT Press, 1994.

van der Nüll, Eduard. "Andeutungen über die kunstgemäße Beziehung des Ornamentes zur rohen Form." *Österreichische Blätter für Literatur und Kunst,* 1845.

Venturi, Robert. *Complexity and Contradiction in Architecture.* 2nd ed. New York: Museum of Modern Art, 1977.

Vidler, Anthony. *The Architectural Uncanny: Essays in the Modern Unhomely.* Rev. ed. Cambridge: MIT Press, 1994.

Vidler, Anthony. *Histories of the Immediate Present: Inventing Architectural Modernism.* Cambridge: MIT Press, 2008.

Viollet-le-Duc, Eugène-Emmanuel. "De la construction des édifices religieux en France." *Annales archéologiques,* 1844.

Vitruvius. *Les Dix Livres d'architecture de Vitruve.* Translated from the Latin by Claude Perrault. Paris, 1684.

Vitruvius. *The Ten Books on Architecture.* Mineola, N.Y.: Dover, 1960.

Wagner, Otto. *Modern Architecture.* Translated by Harry Francis Mallgrave. Santa Monica, Calif.: Getty Center for the History of Art and the Humanities, 1988.

Weir, Simon. "Object Oriented Ontology and the Challenge of the Corinthian Capital." In *Make Sense 2020,* edited by Kate Goodwin and Adrian Thai, 114–16. Sydney: Harvest, 2020.

Weir, Simon. "Salvador Dalí's Interiors with Heraclitus's Concealment." In *The Interior Architecture Theory Reader,* edited by Gregory Marinic, 195–201. London: Routledge, 2018.

Whitehead, Alfred North. *Process and Reality.* New York: Free Press, 1978.

Wigley, Mark. *The Architecture of Deconstruction: Derrida's Haunt.* Cambridge: MIT Press, 1993.

Wiscombe, Tom. "Discreteness, or Towards a Flat Ontology of Architecture." *Project,* no. 3 (2014): 34–43.

Wittgenstein, Ludwig. *Philosophical Investigations.* Translated by G. E. M. Anscombe, P. M. S. Hacker, and Joachim Schulte. London: Wiley-Blackwell, 1989.

Woessner, Martin. *Heidegger in America.* Cambridge: Cambridge University Press, 2011.

Wolfendale, Peter. *Object-Oriented Philosophy: The Noumenon's New Clothes.* Falmouth, England: Urbanomic Media, 2014.

Wright, Frank Lloyd. "The Cardboard House." In *Collected Writings.* Vol. 2, *1930–1932.* New York: Rizzoli, 1992.

Yaneva, Albena. *The Making of a Building: A Pragmatist Approach to Architecture.* New York: Peter Lang, 2009.

Yaneva, Albena, and Brett Mommersteeg. "The Unbearable Lightness of Architectural Aesthetic Discourse." In Gage, *Aesthetics Equals Politics*, 213–33.

Young, Michael. "The Aesthetics of Abstraction." In Gage, *Aesthetics Equals Politics*, 127–48.

Young, Niki. "On Correlationism and the Philosophy of (Human) Access: Meillassoux and Harman." *Open Philosophy* 3 (2020): 42–52.

Žižek, Slavoj. *The Parallax View*. Cambridge: MIT Press, 2006.

Žižek, Slavoj. *The Sublime Object of Ideology*. London: Verso, 1989.

Zumthor, Peter. *Thinking Architecture*. 3rd ed. Basel: Birkhäuser, 2010.

INDEX

GRAHAM HARMAN is Distinguished Professor of Philosophy at the Southern California Institute of Architecture. His books include *Art and Objects* and *Object-Oriented Ontology: A New Theory of Everything.*